The Paris Agreement on Climate Change

By

Mr. Michael C. Enwerem

Table of Content

Preface

Global warming and climate change are terms for the observed century-scale rise in the average temperature of the Earth's climate system and its related effects. Multiple lines of scientific evidence show that the climate system is warming. Although the increase of near-surface atmospheric temperature is the measure of global warming often reported in the popular press, most of the additional energy stored in the climate system since 1970 has gone into ocean warming. The remainder has melted ice and warmed the continents and atmosphere. Many of the observed changes since the 1950s are unprecedented over decades to millennia. Scientific understanding of global warming is increasing. The Intergovernmental Panel on Climate Change (IPCC) reported in 2014 that scientists were more than 95% certain that global warming is mostly being caused by increasing concentrations of greenhouse gases and other human (anthropogenic) activities.

The 2015 United Nations Climate Change Conference, COP 21 or CMP 11 was held in Paris, France, from 30 November to 12 December 2015. It was the 21st yearly session of the Conference of the Parties (COP) to the 1992 United Nations Framework Convention on Climate Change (UNFCCC) and the 11th session of the Meeting of the Parties to the 1997 Kyoto Protocol.

The conference negotiated the Paris Agreement, a global agreement on the reduction of climate change, the text of which represented a consensus of the representatives of the 196 parties attending it. According to the organizing committee at the outset of the talks, the expected key result was an agreement to set a goal of limiting global warming to less than 2 degrees Celsius (°C) compared to pre-industrial levels. The agreement calls for zero net anthropogenic greenhouse gas emissions to be reached during the second half of the 21st century.

Chapter 1

Introduction

Earth has been in radiative imbalance since at least the 1970s, where less energy leaves the atmosphere than enters it. Most of this extra energy has been absorbed by the oceans. It is very likely that human activities substantially contributed to this increase in ocean heat content.

The global average (land and ocean) surface temperature shows a warming of 0.85 [0.65 to 1.06] °C in the period 1880 to 2012, based on multiple independently produced datasets. Earth's average surface temperature rose by 0.74+0.18 °C over the period 1906–2005. The rate of warming almost doubled for the last half of that period (0.13+0.03 °C per decade, versus 0.07±0.02 °C per decade).

The average temperature of the lower troposphere has increased between 0.13 and 0.22 °C (0.23 and 0.40 °F) per decade since 1979, according to satellite temperature measurements. Climate proxies show the temperature to have been relatively stable over the one or two thousand years before 1850, with regionally varying fluctuations such as the Medieval Warm Period and the Little Ice Age.

The warming that is evident in the instrumental temperature record is consistent with a wide range of observations, as documented by many independent scientific groups. Examples include sea level rise, widespread melting of snow and land ice, increased heat content of the oceans, increased humidity, and the earlier timing of spring events, e.g., the flowering of plants. The probability that these changes could have occurred by chance is virtually zero.

Trends

Temperature changes vary over the globe. Since 1979, land temperatures have increased about twice as fast as ocean temperatures (0.25 °C per decade against 0.13 °C per decade).Ocean temperatures increase more slowly than land temperatures because of the larger effective heat capacity of the oceans and because the ocean loses more heat by evaporation. Since the beginning of industrialization the temperature difference between the hemispheres has increased due to melting of sea ice and snow in the North. Average arctic temperatures have been increasing at almost twice the rate of the rest of the world in the past 100 years; however arctic temperatures are also highly variable. Although more greenhouse gases are emitted in the Northern than Southern Hemisphere this does not contribute to the difference in warming because the major greenhouse gases persist long enough to mix between hemispheres.

The thermal inertia of the oceans and slow responses of other indirect effects mean that climate can take centuries or longer to adjust to changes in forcing. Climate commitment studies indicate that even if greenhouse gases were stabilized at year 2000 levels

Global temperature is subject to short-term fluctuations that overlay long-term trends and can temporarily mask them. The relative stability in surface temperature from 2002 to 2009, which has been dubbed the global warming hiatus by the media and some scientists, is consistent with such an episode. Recent updates to account for differing methods of measuring ocean surface temperature measurements show a significant positive trend over the recent decade.

The green-house effect

The climate system can warm or cool in response to changes in external forces. These are "external" to the climate system but not necessarily external to Earth. Examples of external forces include changes in atmospheric composition (e.g., increased concentrations of greenhouse gases), solar luminosity, volcanic eruptions, and variations in Earth's orbit around the Sun.

The greenhouse effect is the process by which absorption and emission of infrared radiation by gases in a planet's atmosphere warm its lower atmosphere and surface. It was proposed by Joseph Fourier in 1824, discovered in 1860 by John Tyndall, was first investigated quantitatively by Svante Arrhenius in 1896, and was developed in the 1930s through 1960s by Guy Stewart Callendar.

On Earth, naturally occurring amounts of greenhouse gases have a mean warming effect of about 33 °C (59 °F). Without the Earth's atmosphere, the Earth's average temperature would be well below the freezing temperature of water. The major greenhouse gases are water vapor, which causes about 36–70% of the greenhouse effect; carbon dioxide (CO_2), which causes 9–26%; methane (CH_4), which causes 4–9%; and ozone (O_3), which causes 3–7%. Clouds also affect the radiation balance through cloud, forcing similar to greenhouse gases.

Human activity since the Industrial Revolution has increased the amount of greenhouse gases in the atmosphere, leading to increased radiative forcing from CO_2, methane, tropospheric ozone, CFCs and nitrous oxide. According to studies published in 2007, the concentrations of CO_2 and methane have increased by 36% and 148% respectively since 1750. These levels are much higher than at any time during the last 800,000 years, the period for which reliable data has been extracted from ice cores. Less direct geological evidence indicates that CO_2 values higher than this were last seen about 20 million years ago. Fossil fuel burning has produced about three-quarters of the increase in CO_2 from human activity over the past 20 years. The rest of this increase is caused mostly by changes in land-use, particularly deforestation. Estimates of global CO_2 emissions in 2011 from fossil fuel combustion, including cement production and gas flaring, was 34.8 billion tonnes (9.5 ± 0.5 PgC), an increase of 54% above emissions in 1990. Coal burning was responsible for 43% of the total emissions, oil 34%, gas 18%, cement 4.9% and gas flaring 0.7%.

In May 2013, it was reported that readings for CO_2 taken at the world's primary benchmark site in Mauna Loa surpassed 400 ppm. According to professor Brian Hoskins 2013, this is likely the first time CO_2 levels have been this high for about 4.5 million years. Monthly global CO_2 concentrations exceeded 400 p.p.m. in March 2015, probably for the first time in several million years.

On 12 November 2015, NASA scientists reported that human-made carbon dioxide (CO_2) continues to increase above levels not seen in hundreds of thousands of years: currently, about half of the carbon dioxide released from the burning of fossil fuels remains in the atmosphere and is not absorbed by vegetation and the oceans.

Over the last three decades of the twentieth century, gross domestic product per capita and population growth were the main drivers of increases in greenhouse gas emissions. CO_2 emissions are continuing to rise due to the burning of fossil fuels and land-use change. Emissions can be attributed to different regions. Attribution of emissions due to land-use change is a controversial issue.

Emissions scenarios, estimates of changes in future emission levels of greenhouse gases, have been projected that depend upon uncertain economic, sociological, technological, and natural developments. In most scenarios, emissions continue to rise over the century, while in a few, emissions are reduced. Fossil fuel reserves are abundant, and will not limit carbon emissions in the 21st century. Emission scenarios, combined with modelling of the carbon cycle, have been used to produce estimates of how atmospheric concentrations of greenhouse gases might change in the future. Using the six IPCC SRES "marker" scenarios, models suggest that by the year 2100, the atmospheric concentration of CO_2 could range between 541 and 970 ppm. This is 90–250% above the concentration in the year 1750.

The popular media and the public often confuse global warming with ozone depletion, i.e., the destruction of stratospheric ozone (e.g., the ozone layer) by chlorofluorocarbons. Although there are a few areas of linkage, the relationship between the two is not strong. Reduced stratospheric ozone has had a slight cooling influence on surface temperatures, while increased tropospheric ozone has had a somewhat larger warming effect.

Ship tracks can be seen as lines in these clouds over the Atlantic Ocean on the east coast of the United States. Atmospheric particles from these and other sources could have a large effect on climate through the aerosol indirect effect.

Global dimming, a gradual reduction in the amount of global direct irradiance at the Earth's surface, was observed from 1961 until at least 1990. Solid and liquid particles known as aerosols, produced by volcanoes and human-made pollutants, are thought to be the main cause of this dimming. They exert a cooling effect by increasing the reflection of incoming sunlight. The effects of the products of fossil fuel combustion – CO_2 and aerosols – have partially offset one another in recent decades, so that net warming has been due to the increase in non-CO_2 greenhouse gases such as methane. Radiative forcing due to aerosols is temporally limited due to the processes that remove aerosols from the atmosphere.

Removal by clouds and precipitation gives tropospheric aerosols an atmospheric lifetime of only about a week, while stratospheric aerosols can remain for a few years. Carbon dioxide has a lifetime of a century or more, and as such, changes in aerosols will only delay climate changes due to carbon dioxide. Black carbon is second only to carbon dioxide for its contribution to global warming.

In addition to their direct effect by scattering and absorbing solar radiation, aerosols have indirect effects on the Earth's radiation budget. Sulfate aerosols act as cloud condensation nuclei and thus lead to clouds that have more and smaller cloud droplets. These clouds reflect solar radiation more efficiently than clouds with fewer and larger droplets, a phenomenon known as the Twomey effect. This effect also causes droplets to be of more uniform size, which reduces growth of raindrops and makes the cloud more reflective to incoming sunlight, known as the Albrecht effect. Indirect effects are most noticeable in marine strati-form clouds, and have very little radiative effect on convective clouds. Indirect effects of aerosols represent the largest uncertainty in radiative forcing.

Soot may either cool or warm Earth's climate system, depending on whether it is airborne or deposited. Atmospheric soot directly absorbs solar radiation, which heats the atmosphere and cools the surface. In isolated areas with high soot production, such as rural India, as much as 50% of surface warming due to greenhouse gases may be masked by atmospheric brown clouds. When deposited, especially on glaciers or on ice in arctic regions, the lower surface albedo can also directly heat the surface. The influences of atmospheric particles, including black carbon, are most pronounced in the tropics and sub-tropics, particularly in Asia, while the effects of greenhouse gases are dominant in the extra-tropics and southern hemisphere.

Contribution of natural factors and human activities to radiative forcing of climate change, Radiative forcing values are for the year 2005, relative to the pre-industrial era. The contribution of solar irradiance to radiative forcing is 5% the value of the combined radiative forcing due to increases in the atmospheric concentrations of carbon dioxide, methane and nitrous oxide.

Solar activity and climate

Since 1978, solar irradiance has been measured by satellites. These measurements indicate that the Sun's radiative output has not increased since 1978, so the warming during the past 30 years cannot be attributed to an increase in solar energy reaching the Earth.

Climate models have been used to examine the role of the Sun in recent climate change. Models are unable to reproduce the rapid warming observed in recent decades when they only take into account variations in solar output and volcanic activity. Models are, however, able to simulate the observed 20th century changes in temperature when they include all of the most important external forces, including human influences and natural forces.

Another line of evidence against the Sun having caused recent climate change comes from looking at how temperatures at different levels in the Earth's atmosphere have changed.

Models and observations show that greenhouse warming results in warming of the lower atmosphere (called the troposphere) but cooling of the upper atmosphere (called the stratosphere). Depletion of the ozone layer by chemical refrigerants has also resulted in a strong cooling effect in the stratosphere.

The tilt of the Earth's axis and the shape of its orbit around the Sun vary slowly over tens of thousands of years and are a natural source of climate change, by changing the seasonal and latitudinal distribution of solar insolation.

During the last few thousand years, this phenomenon contributed to a slow cooling trend at high latitudes of the Northern Hemisphere during summer, a trend that was reversed by greenhouse-gas-induced warming during the 20th century.

Variations in orbital cycles may initiate a new glacial period in the future, though the timing of this depends on greenhouse gas concentrations as well as the orbital forcing. A new glacial period is not expected within the next 50,000 years if atmospheric CO_2 concentration remains above 300 ppm.

Effects of global warming

Anthropogenic forcing has likely contributed to some of the observed changes, including sea level rise, changes in climate extremes (such as the number of warm and cold days), declines in Arctic sea ice extent, glacier retreat, and greening of the Sahara.

During the 21st century, glaciers and snow cover are projected to continue their widespread retreat. Projections of declines in Arctic sea ice vary. Recent projections suggest that Arctic summers could be ice-free (defined as ice extent less than 1 million square km) as early as 2025-2030.

Changes in regional climate are expected to include greater

warming over land, with most warming at high northern latitudes, and least warming over the Southern Ocean and parts of the North Atlantic Ocean.

Future changes in precipitation are expected to follow existing trends, with reduced precipitation over subtropical land areas, and increased precipitation at subpolar latitudes and some equatorial regions. Projections suggest a probable increase in the frequency and severity of some extreme weather events, such as heat waves.

A 2015 study published in Nature, states: About 18% of the moderate daily precipitation extremes over land are attributable to the observed temperature increase since pre-industrial times, which in turn primarily results from human influence. For 2 °C of warming the fraction of precipitation extremes attributable to human influence rises to about 40%. Likewise, today about 75% of the moderate daily hot extremes over land are attributable to warming. It is the most rare and extreme events for which the largest fraction is anthropogenic, and that contribution increases nonlinearly with further warming. .

Sea level rise

Sea level rise has been estimated to be on average +2.6 mm and +2.9 mm per year ± 0.4 mm since 1993. Additionally, sea level rise has accelerated in recent years. Over the 21st century, the IPCC projects for a high emissions scenario, that global mean sea level could rise by 52–98 cm. The IPCC's projections are conservative, and may underestimate future sea level rise. Other estimates suggest for the same period that global mean sea level could rise by 0.2 to 2.0 m (0.7–6.6 ft), relative to mean sea level in 1992.

Widespread coastal flooding would be expected if several degrees of warming are sustained for millennia. For example, sustained global warming of more than 2 °C (relative to pre-industrial levels) could lead to eventual sea level rise of around 1 to

4m due to thermal expansion of sea water and the melting of glaciers and small ice caps. Melting of the Greenland ice sheet could contribute an additional 4 to 7.5m over many thousands of years. It has been estimated that we are already committed to a sea-level rise of approximately 2.3 meters for each degree of temperature rise within the next 2,000 years.

Warming beyond the 2 °C target would potentially lead to rates of sea-level rise dominated by ice loss from Antarctica. Continued CO_2 emissions from fossil sources could cause additional tens of meters of sea level rise, over the next millennia and eventually ultimately eliminate the entire Antarctic ice sheet, causing about 58 meters of sea level rise.

Climate change and ecosystems

In terrestrial ecosystems, the earlier timing of spring events, and poleward and upward shifts in plant and animal ranges, have been linked with high confidence to recent warming. Future climate change is expected to particularly affect certain ecosystems, including tundra, mangroves, and coral reefs. It is expected that most ecosystems will be affected by higher atmospheric CO_2 levels, combined with higher global temperatures. Overall, it is expected that climate change will result in the extinction of many species and reduced diversity of ecosystems.

Increases in atmospheric CO_2 concentrations have led to an increase in ocean acidity. Dissolved CO_2 increases ocean acidity, which is measured by lower pH values.

Between 1750 to 2000, surface-ocean pH has decreased by ≈0.1, from ≈8.2 to ≈8.1. Surface-ocean pH has probably not been below ≈8.1 during the past 2 million years. Projections suggest that surface-ocean pH could decrease by an additional 0.3–0.4 units by 2100. Future ocean acidification could threaten coral reefs, fisheries, protected species, and other natural resources of value to society.

Ocean deoxygenation is projected to increase hypoxia by

10%, and triple suboxic waters (oxygen concentrations 98% less than the mean surface concentrations), for each 1 °C of upper Ocean warming.

On the timescale of centuries to millennia, the magnitude of global warming will be determined primarily by anthropogenic CO_2 emissions. This is due to carbon dioxide's very long lifetime in the atmosphere.

Stabilizing the global average temperature would require large reductions in CO_2 emissions, as well as reductions in emissions of other greenhouse gases such as methane and nitrous oxide. Emissions of CO_2 would need to be reduced by more than 80% relative to their peak level. Even if this were achieved, global average temperatures would remain close to their highest level for many centuries.

Long-term effects also include a response from the Earth's crust, due to ice melting and deglaciation, in a process called post-glacial rebound, when land masses are no longer depressed by the weight of ice. This could lead to landslides and increased seismic and volcanic activities. Tsunamis could be generated by submarine landslides caused by warmer ocean water thawing ocean-floor permafrost or releasing gas hydrates. Some world regions, such as the French Alps, already show signs of an increase in landslide frequency.

Climate change could result in global, large-scale changes in natural and social systems. Two examples are ocean acidification caused by increased atmospheric concentrations of carbon dioxide, and the long-term melting of ice sheets, which contributes to sea level rise.

Some large-scale changes could occur abruptly, i.e., over a short time period, and might also be irreversible. An example of abrupt climate change is the rapid release of methane and carbon dioxide from permafrost, which would lead to amplified global warming. Scientific understanding of abrupt climate change is generally poor. The probability of abrupt change for some climate related feedbacks may be low. Factors that may increase the probability of abrupt climate change include higher magnitudes of global warming, warming that occurs more rapidly, and warming that is sustained over longer time periods.

The effects of climate change on human systems, mostly due to warming or shifts in precipitation patterns, or both, have been detected worldwide. Production of wheat and maize globally has been impacted by climate change. While crop production has increased in some mid-latitude regions such as the UK and Northeast China, economic losses due to extreme weather events have increased globally. There has been a shift from cold- to heat-related mortality in some regions as a result of warming. Livelihoods of indigenous peoples of the Arctic have been altered by climate change, and there is emerging evidence of climate change impacts on livelihoods of indigenous peoples in other regions. Regional impacts of climate change are now observable at more locations than before, on all continents and across ocean regions.

The future social impacts of climate change will be uneven. Many risks are expected to increase with higher magnitudes of global warming. All regions are at risk of experiencing negative impacts. Low-latitude, less developed areas face the greatest risk. A study from 2015 concluded that economic growth (Gross domestic product) of poorer countries is much more impaired with projected future climate warming, than previously thought.

A meta-analysis of 56 studies concluded in 2014 that each degree of temperature rise will increase violence by up to 20%, which includes fist fights, violent crimes, civil unrest or wars. Examples of impacts include, (1) Food; Crop production will probably be negatively affected in low latitude countries, while effects at northern latitudes may be positive or negative; warming of around 4.6 °C relative to pre-industrial levels could pose a large risk to global and regional food security. (2) Health; generally, impacts will be more negative than positive. Impacts include: the effects of extreme weather, leading to injury and loss of life; and indirect effects, such as undernutrition brought on by crop failures.

Chapter 2

The Paris Conference

The purpose of the Paris Conference on climate change is to tackle the issues of climate and global warming as analyzed in chapter 1 of this book to a reasonable and accepted level.

According to the organizing committee of the summit in Paris, the objective of the 2015 conference was to achieve, for the first time in over 20 years of UN negotiations, a binding and universal agreement on climate, from all the nations of the world. Pope Francis published an encyclical called 'Laudato Si' intended, in part, to influence the conference. The encyclical calls for action against climate change. The International Trade Union Confederation before the conference called for the goal to be "zero carbon, zero poverty", and its general secretary Sharan Burrow has repeated that there are "no jobs on a dead planet".

Before the conference, the World Pensions Council (WPC) argued that the keys to success lied in convincing officials in the U.S. and China, by far the two largest national emitters: "As long as policy makers in Washington and Beijing didn't put all their political capital behind the adoption of ambitious carbon-emission capping targets, the laudable efforts of other G20 governments often remained in the realm of pious wishes. Things changed for the better on 12 November 2014 when President Obama and General Secretary Xi Jinping agreed to limit greenhouse gases emissions.

During President Obama speech he insisted on America's essential role in that regard and said, *"We've led by example... from Alaska to the Gulf Coast to the Great Plains... we've seen the longest streak of private job creation in our history. We've driven our economic output to all time-highs while driving our carbon pollution down to its lowest level in nearly two decades. And then, with our historic joint announcement with China last year, we showed it was possible to bridge the old divide between developed and developing nations that had stymied global progress for so long. That was the foundation for success in Paris."*

Location and participation

The 2015 conference was held at Le Bourget Paris from 30 November to 11 December 2015

To some extent, France served as a model country for delegates attending COP21 because it is one of the few developed countries in the world to decarbonize electricity production and fossil fuel energy while still providing a high standard of living. As of 2012, France generated over 90% of its electricity from zero carbon sources, including nuclear, hydroelectric, and wind.

The conference took place two weeks after a series of terrorist attacks in central Paris. Security was tightened accordingly, with 30,000 police officers and 285 security checkpoints deployed across the country until after the conference ended.

The overarching goal of the Convention is to reduce greenhouse gas emissions to limit the global temperature increase. Since COP 17 this increase is set at 2 °C (3.6 °F) above pre-industrial levels.

During previous climate negotiations, countries agreed to outline actions they intended to take within a global agreement, by 1 October 2015. These commitments are known as Intended Nationally Determined Contributions or INDCs. Together, the INDCs would reduce global warming from an estimated 4–5 °C (by 2100) to 2.7 °C, and reduce emissions per capita by 9% by 2030, while providing hope in the eyes of the conference organizers for further reductions in the future that would allow meeting a 2 °C target.

On 12 December 2015, the participating 195 countries agreed, by consensus, to the final global pact, the Paris Agreement, to reduce emissions as part of the method for reducing greenhouse gas. In the 12-page document, the members agreed to reduce their carbon output "*as soon as possible*" and to do their best to keep global warming "*to well below 2 degrees C*". France's Foreign Minister, Laurent Fabius, said this "*ambitious and balanced*" plan was a "*historic turning point*" in the goal of reducing global warming.

The Agreement will not become binding on its member states until 55 parties who produce over 55% of the world's greenhouse gas have ratified the Agreement. There is doubt whether some countries, especially the United States, will agree to do so.

Each country that ratifies the agreement will be required to set a target for emission reduction, but the amount will be voluntary. There will be neither a mechanism to force a country to set a target by a specific date nor enforcement measures if a set target is not met. There will be only a "*name and shame*" system or, as Janos Pasztor, the U.N. assistant secretary-general on climate change, told CBS News , a "*name and encourage*" plan.

Speaking at the 5th annual World Pensions Forum held on the sidelines of the COP21 Summit, Earth Institute Director Jeffrey Sachs argued that institutional investors would eventually divest from carbon-reliant firms if they could not react to political and regulatory efforts to halt climate change: "*Every energy company in a pension fund 's portfolio needs to be scrutinized from purely a financial view about its future, 'Why is this [a company] we would want to hold over a five- to 20-year period?'*... If we continue to hold major energy companies that don't have an answer to a basic financial test, we are just gambling. We have to take a fiduciary responsibility – these are not good bets."

Some US policy makers concurred, notably Al Gore, insisting that "*no agreement is perfect, and this one must be strengthened over time, but groups across every sector of society will now begin to reduce dangerous carbon pollution through the framework of this agreement.*"

Chapter 3

Summary of the Paris Agreement

The Paris Agreement is an agreement within the framework of the United Nations Framework Convention on Climate Change (UNFCCC) governing carbon dioxide reduction measures from 2020. The agreement was negotiated during the 21st Conference of the Parties of the UNFCCC in Paris as stated in Chapter 2 of this book, and adopted by consensus on 12 December 2015, but has not entered into force.

The aim of the convention is described in Article 2, *"enhancing the implementation"* of the UNFCC through:

"(1) Holding the increase in the global average temperature to well below 2 °C above pre-industrial levels and to pursue efforts to limit the temperature increase to 1.5 °C above pre-industrial levels, recognizing that this would significantly reduce the risks and impacts of climate change;

(2) Increasing the ability to adapt to the adverse impacts of climate change and foster climate resilience and low greenhouse gas emissions development, in a manner that does not threaten food production;

(3) Making finance flows consistent with a pathway towards low greenhouse gas emissions and climate-resilient development."

Countries furthermore aim to reach "global peaking of greenhouse gas emissions as soon as possible".

Nationally Determined Contributions (NDCs)

The contribution that each individual country should make in order to achieve the worldwide goal are determined by all countries individually and called "nationally determined contributions"

The Agreement requires them to be "*ambitious*" and set "*with the view to achieving the purpose of this Agreement*". The contributions should be reported every five years and are to be registered by the UNFCCC Secretariat. Each further ambition should be more ambitious than the previous one. Countries can cooperate and pool their nationally determined contributions. The Intended Nationally Determined Contributions pledged during the 2015 Climate Change Conference serve—unless provided otherwise—as the initial nationally determined contribution.

The level of NDCs set by each country will set with binding targets as is the case in the Kyoto protocol. Furthermore, there will be no mechanism to force a country to set a target in their NDC by a specific date and no enforcement if a set target in an NDC is not met. [5][8] There will be only a "name and shame" system or as Janos Pasztor, the U.N. assistant secretary-general on climate change, told CBS News (US), a "name and encourage" plan.

The implementation of the agreement by all member countries together will be evaluated every 5 years, with the first evaluation in 2023. The outcome is to be used as input for new nationally determined contributions of member states. The stocktake will not be of contributions/achievements of individual countries but a collective analysis of what has been achieved and what more needs to be done.

Adoption of the agreement

Within the United Nations Framework Convention on Climate Change, legal instruments may be adopted to reach the goals

the convention. For the period from 2008 to 2012, greenhouse gas reduction measures were agreed in the Kyoto Protocol in 1997. The scope of the protocol was extended until 2020 with the Doha Amendment to that protocol in 2012.

During the 2011 United Nations Climate Change Conference, the Durban Platform (and the Ad Hoc Working Group on the Durban Platform for Enhanced Action) was established with the aim to negotiate a legal instrument governing climate change mitigation measures from 2020.

At the conclusion of COP 21, on 12 December 2015, the final wording of the Paris Agreement was adopted by consensus by all of the 195 UNFCCC participating member states and the European Union to reduce emissions as part of the method for reducing greenhouse gas. In the 12 page Agreement, the members promised to reduce their carbon output *"as soon as possible"* and to do their best to keep global warming *"to well below 2 degrees C"* (3.6 degrees F). The agreement indicates a (non-binding) plan to provide $100 billion a year in aid to developing countries for implementing new procedures to minimize climate change with additional amounts to be provided in subsequent years.

Entry into force

The agreement will open for signature in April 2016 to all 197 parties of the UNFCCC: all members of the United Nations, as well as Cook Islands, Niue, Palestine and the European Union. It will enter into force (and thus become fully effective) only if 55 countries that produce at least 55% of the world's greenhouse gas emissions ratify the agreement.

It is not known which countries will sign and or ratify. For example, although Democratic US President Barack Obama praised the pact as "*ambitious*" and "*historic*", the Republican-dominated

United States Congress may not ratify it.

Similarly, the conservative Liberal government of Australia has treated climate change with much skepticism particularly under the previous Prime Minister Tony Abbott's leadership.

Chapter 4

Full Test of the Paris Agreement

ADOPTION OF THE PARIS AGREEMENT

Welcoming the adoption of United Nations General Assembly resolution A/RES/70/1, "Transforming our world: the 2030 Agenda for Sustainable Development", in particular its goal 13, and the adoption of the Addis Ababa Action Agenda of the third International Conference on Financing for Development and the adoption of the Sendai Framework for Disaster Risk Reduction,

Recognizing that climate change represents an urgent and potentially irreversible threat to human societies and the planet and thus requires the widest possible cooperation by all countries, and their participation in an effective and appropriate international response, with a view to accelerating the reduction of global greenhouse gas emissions,

Also recognizing that deep reductions in global emissions will be required in order to achieve the ultimate objective of the Convention and emphasizing the need for urgency in addressing climate change,

Acknowledging that climate change is a common concern of humankind, Parties should, when taking action to address climate change, respect, promote and consider their respective obligations on human rights, the right to health, the rights of indigenous peoples, local communities, migrants, children, persons with disabilities and people in vulnerable situations and the right to development, as well as gender equality, empowerment of women and intergenerational equity,

Emphasizing with serious concern the urgent need to address the significant gap between the aggregate effect of Parties' mitigation pledges in terms of global annual emissions of greenhouse gases by 2020 and aggregate emission pathways consistent with holding the increase in the global average temperature to well below 2 °C above pre-industrial levels and efforts to limit the temperature increase to 1.5 °C above pre-industrial levels,

Also emphasizing that enhanced pre-2020 ambition can lay a solid foundation for enhanced post-2020 ambition,

Stressing the urgency of accelerating the implementation of the Convention and its Kyoto Protocol in order to enhance pre-2020 ambition,

Recognizing the urgent need to enhance the provision of finance, technology and capacity-building support by developed country Parties, in a predictable manner, to enable enhanced pre-2020 action by developing country Parties,

Emphasizing the enduring benefits of ambitious and early action, including major reductions in the cost of future mitigation and adaptation efforts,

Acknowledging the need to promote universal access to sustainable energy in developing countries, in particular in Africa, through the enhanced deployment of renewable energy,

Agreeing to uphold and promote regional and international cooperation in order to mobilize stronger and more ambitious climate action by all Parties and non-Party stakeholders, including civil society, the private sector, financial institutions, cities and other subnational authorities, local communities and indigenous peoples,

ADOPTION

1. Decides to adopt the Paris Agreement under the United Nations Framework Convention on Climate Change (hereinafter referred to as "the Agreement") as contained in the annex;

2. Requests the Secretary-General of the United Nations to be the Depositary of the Agreement and to have it open for signature in New York, United States of America, from 22 April 2016 to 21

April 2017;

3. Invites the Secretary-General to convene a high-level signature ceremony for the Agreement on 22 April 2016;

4. Also invites all Parties to the Convention to sign the Agreement at the ceremony to be convened by the Secretary-General, or at their earliest opportunity, and to deposit their respective instruments of ratification, acceptance, approval or accession, where appropriate, as soon as possible;

5. Recognizes that Parties to the Convention may provisionally apply all of the provisions of the Agreement pending its entry into force, and requests Parties to provide notification of any such provisional application to the Depositary;

6. Notes that the work of the Ad Hoc Working Group on the Durban Platform for Enhanced Action, in accordance with decisions has been completed;

7. Decides to establish the Ad Hoc Working Group on the Paris Agreement under the same arrangement, mutatis mutandis, as those concerning the election of officers to the Bureau of the Ad Hoc Working Group on the Durban Platform for Enhanced Action;1

8. Also decides that the Ad Hoc Working Group on the Paris Agreement shall prepare for the entry into force of the Agreement and for the convening of the first session of the Conference of the Parties serving as the meeting of the Parties to the Paris Agreement;

9. Further decides to oversee the implementation of the work programme resulting from the relevant requests contained in this decision;

10. Requests the Ad Hoc Working Group on the Paris Agreement to report regularly to the Conference of the Parties on the

progress of its work and to complete its work by the first session of the Conference of the Parties serving as the meeting of the Parties to the Paris Agreement;

11. Decides that the Ad Hoc Working Group on the Paris Agreement shall hold its sessions starting in 2016 in conjunction with the sessions of the Convention subsidiary bodies and shall prepare draft decisions to be recommended through the Conference of the Parties to the Conference of the Parties serving as the meeting of the Parties to the Paris Agreement for consideration and adoption at its first session;

INTENDED NATIONALLY DETERMINED CONTRIBUTIONS

12. Welcomes the intended nationally determined contributions that have been communicated by Parties in accordance with decision.

13. Reiterates its invitation to all Parties that have not yet done so to communicate to the secretariat their intended nationally determined contributions towards achieving the objective of the Convention as set out in its Article 2 as soon as possible and well in advance of the twenty-second session of the Conference of the Parties (November 2016) and in a manner that facilitates the clarity, transparency and understanding of the intended nationally determined contributions;

14. Requests the secretariat to continue to publish the intended nationally determined contributions communicated by Parties on the UNFCCC website;

15. Reiterates its call to developed country Parties, the operating entities of the Financial Mechanism and any other organizations in a position to do so to provide support for the preparation and communication of the intended nationally

determined contributions of Parties that may need such support;

16. Takes note of the synthesis report on the aggregate effect of intended nationally determined contributions communicated by Parties by 1 October 2015.

17. Notes with concern that the estimated aggregate greenhouse gas emission levels in 2025 and 2030 resulting from the intended nationally determined contributions do not fall within least-cost 2 °C scenarios but rather lead to a projected level of 55 gigatonnes in 2030, and also notes that much greater emission reduction efforts will be required than those associated with the intended nationally determined contributions in order to hold the increase in the global average temperature to below 2 °C above pre-industrial levels by reducing emissions to 40 gigatonnes or to 1.5 °C above pre-industrial levels by reducing to a level to be identified in the special report of the document.

18. Also notes, in this context, the adaptation needs expressed by many developing country Parties in their intended nationally determined contributions;

19. Requests the secretariat to update the synthesis report referred to in paragraph 16 above so as to cover all the information in the intended nationally determined contributions communicated by Parties pursuant to decision 1/CP.20 by 4 April 2016 and to make it available by 2 May 2016;

20. Decides to convene a facilitative dialogue among Parties in 2018 to take stock of the collective efforts of Parties in relation to progress towards the long-term goal referred to in Article 4, paragraph 1, of the Agreement and to inform the preparation of nationally determined contributions pursuant to Article 4, paragraph 8, of the Agreement;

21. Invites the Intergovernmental Panel on Climate Change to provide a special report in 2018 on the impacts of global warming of 1.5 °C above pre-industrial levels and related global greenhouse gas emission pathways;

DECISIONS TO GIVE EFFECT TO THE AGREEMENT MITIGATION

22. Invites Parties to communicate their first nationally determined contribution no later than when the Party submits its respective instrument of ratification, accession, or approval of the Paris Agreement. If a Party has communicated an intended nationally determined contribution prior to joining the Agreement, that Party shall be considered to have satisfied this provision unless that Party decides otherwise;

23. Urges those Parties whose intended nationally determined contribution pursuant to decision 1/CP.20 contains a time frame up to 2025 to communicate by 2020 a new nationally determined contribution and to do so every five years thereafter pursuant to Article 4, paragraph 9, of the Agreement;

24. Requests those Parties whose intended nationally determined contribution pursuant to decision 1/CP.20 contains a time frame up to 2030 to communicate or update by 2020 these contributions and to do so every five years thereafter pursuant to Article 4, paragraph 9, of the Agreement;

25. Decides that Parties shall submit to the secretariat their nationally determined contributions referred to in Article 4 of the Agreement at least 9 to 12 months in advance of the relevant meeting of the Conference of the Parties serving as the meeting of the Parties to the Paris Agreement with a view to facilitating the clarity, transparency and understanding of these contributions, including through a synthesis report prepared by the secretariat;

26. Requests the Ad Hoc Working Group on the Paris Agreement to develop further guidance on features of the nationally determined contributions for consideration and adoption by the Conference of the Parties serving as the meeting of the Parties to the Paris Agreement at its first session;

27. Agrees that the information to be provided by Parties communicating their nationally determined contributions, in order to facilitate clarity, transparency and understanding, may include, as appropriate, inter alia, quantifiable information on the reference point (including, as appropriate, a base year), time frames and/ or periods for implementation, scope and coverage, planning processes, assumptions and methodological approaches including those for estimating and accounting for anthropogenic greenhouse gas emissions and, as appropriate, removals, and how the Party considers that its nationally determined contribution is fair and ambitious, in the light of its national circumstances, and how it contributes towards achieving the objective of the Convention as set out in its Article

28. Requests the Ad Hoc Working Group on the Paris Agreement to develop further guidance for the information to be provided by Parties in order to facilitate clarity, transparency and understanding of nationally determined contributions for consideration and adoption by the Conference of the Parties serving as the meeting of the Parties to the Paris Agreement at its first session;

29. Also requests the Subsidiary Body for Implementation to develop modalities and procedures for the operation and use of the public registry referred to in Article 4, paragraph 12, of the Agreement, for consideration and adoption by the Conference of the Parties serving as the meeting of the Parties to the Paris Agreement at its first session;

30. Further requests the secretariat to make available an interim public registry in the first half of 2016 for the recording of nationally determined contributions submitted in accordance with Article 4 of the Agreement, pending the adoption by the Conference of the Parties serving as the meeting of the Parties to the Paris Agreement of the modalities and procedures referred to in paragraph 29 above;

31. Requests the Ad Hoc Working Group on the Paris Agreement to elaborate, drawing from approaches established under the Convention and its related legal instruments as appropriate, guidance for accounting for Parties' nationally determined contributions, as referred to in Article 4, paragraph 13, of the Agreement, for consideration and adoption by the Conference of the Parties serving as the meeting of the Parties to the Paris Agreement at its first session, which ensures that:

(a) Parties account for anthropogenic emissions and removals in accordance with methodologies and common metrics assessed by the Intergovernmental Panel on Climate Change and adopted by the Conference of the Parties serving as the meeting of the Parties to the Paris Agreement;

(b) Parties ensure methodological consistency, including on baselines, between the communication and implementation of nationally determined contributions;

(c) Parties strive to include all categories of anthropogenic emissions or removals in their nationally determined contributions and, once a source, sink or activity is included, continue to include it;

(d) Parties shall provide an explanation of why any categories of anthropogenic emissions or removals are excluded;

32. Decides that Parties shall apply the guidance mentioned in paragraph 31 above to the second and subsequent nationally determined contributions and that Parties may elect to apply such guidance to their first nationally determined contribution;

33. Also decides that the Forum on the Impact of the Implementation of response measures, under the subsidiary bodies, shall continue, and shall serve the Agreement;

34. Further decides that the Subsidiary Body for Scientific and Technological Advice and the Subsidiary Body for Implementation shall recommend, for consideration and adoption by the Conference of the Parties serving as the meeting of the Parties to the Paris Agreement at its first session, the modalities, work programme and functions of the Forum on the Impact of the Implementation of response measures to address the effects of the implementation of response measures under the Agreement by enhancing cooperation amongst Parties on understanding the impacts of mitigation actions under the Agreement and the exchange of information, experiences, and best practices amongst Parties to raise their resilience to these impacts;

36. Invites Parties to communicate, by 2020, to the secretariat mid-century, long-term low greenhouse gas emission development strategies in accordance with Article 4, paragraph 19, of the Agreement, and requests the secretariat to publish on the UNFCCC website Parties' low greenhouse gas emission development strategies as communicated;

37. Requests the Subsidiary Body for Scientific and Technological Advice to develop and recommend the guidance referred to under Article 6, paragraph 2, of the Agreement for adoption by the Conference of the Parties serving as the meeting of the Parties to the Paris Agreement at its first session, including guidance to ensure that double counting is avoided on the basis of a corresponding adjustment by Parties for both anthropogenic emissions by sources and removals by sinks covered by their nationally determined contributions under the Agreement;

38. Recommends that the Conference of the Parties serving as the meeting of the Parties to the Paris Agreement adopt rules, modalities and procedures for the mechanism established by Article 6, paragraph 4, of the Agreement on the basis of:

(a) Voluntary participation authorized by each Party involved;

(b) Real, measurable, and long-term benefits related to the mitigation of climate change;

(c) Specific scopes of activities;

(d) Reductions in emissions that are additional to any that would otherwise occur;

(e) Verification and certification of emission reductions resulting from mitigation activities by designated operational entities;

(f) Experience gained with and lessons learned from existing mechanisms and approaches adopted under the Convention and its related legal instruments;

39. Requests the Subsidiary Body for Scientific and Technological Advice to develop and recommend rules, modalities and procedures for the mechanism referred to in paragraph 38 above for consideration and adoption by the Conference of the Parties serving as the meeting of the Parties to the Paris Agreement at its first session;

40. Also requests the Subsidiary Body for Scientific and Technological Advice to undertake a work programme under the framework for non-market approaches to sustainable development referred to in Article 6, paragraph 8, of the Agreement, with the

objective of considering how to enhance linkages and create synergy between, inter alia, mitigation, adaptation, finance, technology transfer and capacity-building, and how to facilitate the implementation and coordination of non-market approaches;

41. Further requests the Subsidiary Body for Scientific and Technological Advice to recommend a draft decision on the work programme referred to in paragraph 40 above, taking into account the views of Parties, for consideration and adoption by the Conference of the Parties serving as the meeting of the Parties to the Paris Agreement at its first session;

ADAPTATION

42. Requests the Adaptation Committee and the Least Developed Countries Expert Group to jointly develop modalities to recognize the adaptation efforts of developing country Parties, as referred to in Article 7, paragraph 3, of the Agreement, and make recommendations for consideration and adoption by the Conference of the Parties serving as the meeting of the Parties to the Paris Agreement at its first session;

43. Also requests the Adaptation Committee, taking into account its mandate and its second three-year workplan, and with a view to preparing recommendations for consideration and adoption by the Conference of the Parties serving as the meeting of the Parties to the Paris Agreement at its first session:

(a) To review, in 2017, the work of adaptation-related institutional arrangements under the Convention, with a view to identifying ways to enhance the coherence of their work, as appropriate, in order to respond adequately to the needs of Parties;

(b) To consider methodologies for assessing adaptation needs with a view to assisting developing countries, without placing an undue burden on them;

44. Invites all relevant United Nations agencies and

international, regional and national financial institutions to provide information to Parties through the secretariat on how their development assistance and climate finance programmes incorporate climate-proofing and climate resilience measures;

45. Requests Parties to strengthen regional cooperation on adaptation where appropriate and, where necessary, establish regional centres and networks, in particular in developing countries, taking into account decision 1/CP.16, paragraph 13;

46. Also requests the Adaptation Committee and the Least Developed Countries Expert Group, in collaboration with the Standing Committee on Finance and other relevant institutions, to develop methodologies, and make recommendations for consideration and adoption by the Conference of the Parties serving as the meeting of the Parties to the Paris Agreement at its first session on:

(a) Taking the necessary steps to facilitate the mobilization of support for adaptation in developing countries in the context of the limit to global average temperature increase referred to in Article 2 of the Agreement;

(b) Reviewing the adequacy and effectiveness of adaptation and support referred to in Article 7, paragraph 14(c), of the Agreement;

47. Further requests the Green Climate Fund to expedite support for the least developed countries and other developing country Parties for the formulation of national adaptation plans, consistent with decisions 1/CP.16 and 5/CP.17, and for the subsequent implementation of policies, projects and programmes identified by them;

LOSS AND DAMAGE

48. Decides on the continuation of the Warsaw International Mechanism for Loss and Damage associated with Climate Change Impacts, following the review in 2016;

49. Requests the Executive Committee of the Warsaw International Mechanism to establish a clearinghouse for risk transfer that serves as a repository for information on insurance and risk transfer, in order to facilitate the efforts of Parties to develop and implement comprehensive risk management strategies;

50. Also requests the Executive Committee of the Warsaw International Mechanism to establish, according to its procedures and mandate, a task force to complement, draw upon the work of and involve, as appropriate, existing bodies and expert groups under the Convention including the Adaptation Committee and the Least Developed Countries Expert Group, as well as relevant organizations and expert bodies outside the Convention, to develop recommendations for integrated approaches to avert, minimize and address displacement related to the adverse impacts of climate change;

51. Further requests the Executive Committee of the Warsaw International Mechanism to initiate its work, at its next meeting, to operationalize the provisions referred to in paragraphs 49 and 50 above, and to report on progress thereon in its annual report;

52. Agrees that Article 8 of the Agreement does not involve or provide a basis for any liability or compensation;

FINANCE

53. Decides that, in the implementation of the Agreement, financial resources provided to developing countries should enhance the implementation of their policies, strategies, regulations and action plans and their climate change actions with respect to both mitigation and adaptation to contribute to the achievement of the purpose of the Agreement as defined in Article 2;

54. Also decides that, in accordance with Article 9, paragraph 3, of the Agreement, developed countries intend to continue their existing collective mobilization goal through 2025 in the context of meaningful mitigation actions and transparency on implementation; prior to 2025 the Conference of the Parties serving as the meeting of the Parties to the Paris Agreement shall set a new collective quantified goal from a floor of USD 100 billion per year, taking into account the needs and priorities of developing countries;

55. Recognizes the importance of adequate and predictable financial resources, including for results-based payments, as appropriate, for the implementation of policy approaches and positive incentives for reducing emissions from deforestation and forest degradation, and the role of conservation, sustainable management of forests and enhancement of forest carbon stocks; as well as alternative policy approaches, such as joint mitigation and adaptation approaches for the integral and sustainable management of forests; while reaffirming the importance of non-carbon benefits associated with such approaches; encouraging the coordination of support from, inter alia, public and private, bilateral and multilateral sources, such as the Green Climate Fund, and alternative sources in accordance with relevant decisions by the Conference of the Parties;

56. Decides to initiate, at its twenty-second session, a process to identify the information to be provided by Parties, in accordance with Article 9, paragraph 5, of the Agreement with the view to providing a recommendation for consideration and adoption by the Conference of the Parties serving as the meeting of the Parties to the Paris Agreement at its first session;

57. Also decides to ensure that the provision of information in accordance with Article 9, paragraph 7 of the Agreement shall be undertaken in accordance with modalities, procedures and guidelines referred to in paragraph 96 below;

58. Requests Subsidiary Body for Scientific and Technological Advice to develop modalities for the accounting of financial resources provided and mobilized through public interventions in accordance with Article 9, paragraph 7, of the Agreement for consideration by the Conference of the Parties at its twenty-fourth session (November 2018), with the view to making a recommendation for consideration and adoption by the Conference of the Parties serving as the meeting of the Parties to the Paris Agreement at its first session;

59. Decides that the Green Climate Fund and the Global Environment Facility, the entities entrusted with the operation of the Financial Mechanism of the Convention, as well as the Least Developed Countries Fund and the Special Climate Change Fund, administered by the Global Environment Facility, shall serve the Agreement;

60. Recognizes that the Adaptation Fund may serve the Agreement, subject to relevant decisions by the Conference of the Parties serving as the meeting of the Parties to the Kyoto Protocol and the Conference of the Parties serving as the meeting of the Parties to the Paris Agreement;

61. Invites the Conference of the Parties serving as the meeting of the Parties to the Kyoto Protocol to consider the issue referred to in paragraph 60 above and make a recommendation to the Conference of the Parties serving as the meeting of the Parties to the Paris Agreement at its first session;

62. Recommends that the Conference of the Parties serving as the meeting of the Parties to the Paris Agreement shall provide guidance to the entities entrusted with the operation of the Financial Mechanism of the Convention on the policies, programme priorities and eligibility criteria related to the Agreement for transmission by the Conference of the Parties;

63. Decides that the guidance to the entities entrusted with the operations of the Financial Mechanism of the Convention in relevant decisions of the Conference of the Parties, including those agreed before adoption of the Agreement, shall apply mutatis mutandis;

64. Also decides that the Standing Committee on Finance shall serve the Agreement in line with its functions and responsibilities established under the Conference of the Parties;

65. Urges the institutions serving the Agreement to enhance the coordination and delivery of resources to support country-driven strategies through simplified and efficient application and approval procedures, and through continued readiness support to developing country Parties, including the least developed countries and small island developing States, as appropriate;

66. Takes note of the interim report of the Technology Executive Committee on guidance on enhanced implementation of the results of technology needs assessments as referred to in document FCCC/SB/2015/INF.3;

67. Decides to strengthen the Technology Mechanism and requests the Technology Executive Committee and the Climate Technology Centre and Network, in supporting the implementation of the Agreement, to undertake further work relating to, inter alia:

(a) Technology research, development and demonstration;
(b) The development and enhancement of endogenous capacities and technologies;

68. Requests the Subsidiary Body for Scientific and Technological Advice to initiate, at its forty-fourth session (May 2016), the elaboration of the technology framework established

under Article 10, paragraph 4, of the Agreement and to report on its findings to the Conference of the Parties, with a view to the Conference of the Parties making a recommendation on the framework to the Conference of the Parties serving as the meeting of the Parties to the Paris Agreement for consideration and adoption at its first session, taking into consideration that the framework should facilitate, inter alia:

(a) The undertaking and updating of technology needs assessments, as well as the enhanced implementation of their results, particularly technology action plans and project ideas, through the preparation of bankable projects;

(b) The provision of enhanced financial and technical support for the implementation of the results of the technology needs assessments;

(c) The assessment of technologies that are ready for transfer;

(d) The enhancement of enabling environments for and the addressing of barriers to the development and transfer of socially and environmentally sound technologies;

69. Decides that the Technology Executive Committee and the Climate Technology Centre and Network shall report to the Conference of the Parties serving as the meeting of the Parties to the Paris Agreement, through the subsidiary bodies, on their activities to support the implementation of the Agreement;

70. Also decides to undertake a periodic assessment of the effectiveness of and the adequacy of the support provided to the Technology Mechanism in supporting the implementation of the Agreement on matters relating to technology development and transfer;

71. Requests the Subsidiary Body for Implementation to initiate, at its forty-fourth session , the elaboration of the scope of and modalities for the periodic assessment referred to in paragraph 70 above, taking into account the review of the Climate Technology

Centre and Network as referred to in decision 2/CP.17, annex VII, paragraph 20 and the modalities for the global stocktake referred to in Article 14 of the Agreement, for consideration and adoption by the Conference of the Parties at its twenty-fifth session (November 2019);

CAPACITY-BUILDING

72. Decides to establish the Paris Committee on Capacity-building whose aim will be to address gaps and needs, both current and emerging, in implementing capacity-building in developing country Parties and further enhancing capacity-building efforts, including with regard to coherence and coordination in capacity-building activities under the Convention;

73. Also decides that the Paris Committee on Capacity-building will manage and oversee the work plan mentioned in paragraph 74 below;

74. Further decides to launch a work plan for the period 2016–2020 with the following activities:

(a) Assessing how to increase synergies through cooperation and avoid duplication among existing bodies established under the Convention that implement capacity-building activities, including through collaborating with institutions under and outside the Convention;

(b) Identifying capacity gaps and needs and recommending ways to address them;

(c) Promoting the development and dissemination of tools and methodologies for the implementation of capacity-building;

(d) Fostering global, regional, national and subnational cooperation;

(e) Identifying and collecting good practices, challenges, experiences, and lessons learned from work on capacity-building by bodies established under the Convention;

(f) Exploring how developing country Parties can take ownership of building and maintaining capacity over time and space;

(g) Identifying opportunities to strengthen capacity at the national, regional, and subnational level;

(h) Fostering dialogue, coordination, collaboration and coherence among relevant processes and initiatives under the Convention, including through exchanging information on capacity-building activities and strategies of bodies established under the Convention;

(i) Providing guidance to the secretariat on the maintenance and further development of the web-based capacity-building portal;

75. Decides that the Paris Committee on Capacity-building will annually focus on an area or theme related to enhanced technical exchange on capacity-building, with the purpose of maintaining up-to-date knowledge on the successes and challenges in building capacity effectively in a particular area;

76. Requests the Subsidiary Body for Implementation to organize annual in-session meetings of the Paris Committee on Capacity-building;

77. Also requests the Subsidiary Body for Implementation to develop the terms of reference for the Paris Committee on Capacity-building, in the context of the third comprehensive review of the implementation of the capacity-building framework, also taking into account paragraphs 75, 76, 77 and 78 above and paragraphs 82 and 83 below, with a view to recommending a draft decision on this matter for consideration and adoption by the Conference of the Parties at its twenty-second session;

78. Invites Parties to submit their views on the membership of the Paris Committee on Capacity-building by 9 March 2016;2

79. Requests the secretariat to compile the submissions

referred to in paragraph 78 above into a miscellaneous document for consideration by the Subsidiary Body for Implementation at its forty-fourth session;

80. Decides that the inputs to the Paris Committee on Capacity-building will include, inter alia, submissions, the outcome of the third comprehensive review of the implementation of the capacity-building framework, the secretariat's annual synthesis report on the implementation of the framework for capacity-building in developing countries, the secretariat's compilation and synthesis report on capacity-building work of bodies established under the Convention and its Kyoto Protocol, and reports on the Durban Forum and the capacity-building portal;

81. Requests the Paris Committee on Capacity-building to prepare annual technical progress reports on its work, and to make these reports available at the sessions of the Subsidiary Body for Implementation coinciding with the sessions of the Conference of the Parties;

82. Also requests the Conference of the Parties at its twenty-fifth session (November 2019), to review the progress, need for extension, the effectiveness and enhancement of the Paris Committee on Capacity-building and to take any action it considers appropriate, with a view to making recommendations to the Conference of the Parties serving as the meeting of the Parties to the Paris Agreement at its first session on enhancing institutional arrangements for capacity-building consistent with Article 11, paragraph 5, of the Agreement;

83. Calls upon all Parties to ensure that education, training and public awareness, as reflected in Article 6 of the Convention and in Article 12 of the Agreement are adequately considered in their contribution to capacity-building;

84. Invites the Conference of the Parties serving as the meeting of the Parties to the Paris Agreement at its first session to explore ways of enhancing the implementation ofntraining, public awareness, public participation and public access to information so as to enhance actions under the Agreement;

TRANSPARENCY OF ACTION AND SUPPORT

85. Decides to establish a Capacity-building Initiative for Transparency in order to build institutional and technical capacity, both pre- and post-2020. This initiative will support developing country Parties, upon request, in meeting enhanced transparency requirements as defined in Article 13 of the Agreement in a timely manner;

86. Also decides that the Capacity-building Initiative for Transparency will aim:
(a) To strengthen national institutions for transparency-related activities in line with national priorities;
(b) To provide relevant tools, training and assistance for meeting the provisions stipulated in Article 13 of the Agreement;
(c) To assist in the improvement of transparency over time;

87. Urges and requests the Global Environment Facility to make arrangements to support the establishment and operation of the Capacity-building Initiative for Transparency as a priority reporting-related need, including through voluntary contributions to support developing countries in the sixth replenishment of the Global Environment Facility and future replenishment cycles, to complement existing support under the Global Environment Facility;

88. Decides to assess the implementation of the Capacity-building Initiative for Transparency in the context of the seventh review of the financial mechanism;

89. Requests that the Global Environment Facility, as an operating entity of the financial mechanism include in its annual report to the Conference of the Parties the progress of work in the design, development and implementation of the Capacity-building Initiative for Transparency referred to in paragraph 85 above starting in 2016;

90. Decides that, in accordance with Article 13, paragraph 2, of the Agreement, developing countries shall be provided flexibility in the implementation of the provisions of that Article, including in the scope, frequency and level of detail of reporting, and in the scope of review, and that the scope of review could provide for in-country reviews to be optional, while such flexibilities shall be reflected in the development of modalities, procedures and guidelines referred to in paragraph 92 below;

91. Also decides that all Parties, except for the least developed country Parties and small island developing States, shall submit the information referred to in Article 13, paragraphs 7, 8, 9 and 10, as appropriate, no less frequently than on a biennial basis, and that the least developed country Parties and small island developing States may submit this information at their discretion;

92. Requests the Ad Hoc Working Group on the Paris Agreement to develop recommendations for modalities, procedures and guidelines in accordance with Article 13, paragraph 13, of the Agreement, and to define the year of their first and subsequent review and update, as appropriate, at regular intervals, for consideration by the Conference of the Parties, at its twenty-fourth session, with a view to forwarding them to the Conference of the Parties serving as the meeting of the Parties to the Paris Agreement for adoption at its first session;

93. Also requests the Ad Hoc Working Group on the Paris Agreement in developing the recommendations for the modalities,

procedures and guidelines referred to in paragraph 92 above to take into account, inter alia:

(a) The importance of facilitating improved reporting and transparency over time;

(b) The need to provide flexibility to those developing country Parties that need it in the light of their capacities;

(c) The need to promote transparency, accuracy, completeness, consistency, and comparability;

(d) The need to avoid duplication as well as undue burden on Parties and the secretariat;

(e) The need to ensure that Parties maintain at least the frequency and quality of reporting in accordance with their respective obligations under the Convention;

(f) The need to ensure that double counting is avoided;

(g) The need to ensure environmental integrity;

94. Further requests the Ad Hoc Working Group on the Paris Agreement, when developing the modalities, procedures and guidelines referred to in paragraph 92 above, to draw on the experiences from and take into account other on-going relevant processes under the Convention;

95. Requests the Ad Hoc Working Group on the Paris Agreement, when developing modalities, procedures and guidelines referred to in paragraph 92 above, to consider, inter alia:

(a) The types of flexibility available to those developing countries that need it on the basis of their capacities;

(b) The consistency between the methodology communicated in the nationally determined contribution and the methodology for reporting on progress made towards achieving individual Parties' respective nationally determined contribution;

(c) That Parties report information on adaptation action and planning including, if appropriate, their national adaptation plans, with a view to collectively exchanging information and sharing lessons learned;

(d) Support provided, enhancing delivery of support for both adaptation and mitigation through, inter alia, the common tabular formats for reporting support, and taking into account issues considered by the Subsidiary Body for Scientific and Technological Advice on methodologies for reporting on financial information, and enhancing the reporting by developing countries on support received, including the use, impact and estimated results thereof;

(e) Information in the biennial assessments and other reports of the Standing Committee on Finance and other relevant bodies under the Convention;

(f) Information on the social and economic impact of response measures;

96. Also requests the Ad Hoc Working Group on the Paris Agreement, when developing recommendations for modalities, procedures and guidelines referred to in paragraph 92 above, to enhance the transparency of support provided in accordance with Article 9 of the Agreement;

97. Further requests the Ad Hoc Working Group on the Paris Agreement to report on the progress of work on the modalities, procedures and guidelines referred to in paragraph

92 above to future sessions of the Conference of the Parties, and that this work be concluded no later than 2018;

98. Decides that the modalities, procedures and guidelines developed under paragraph 92 above, shall be applied upon the entry into force of the Paris Agreement;

99. Also decides that the modalities, procedures and guidelines of this transparency framework shall build upon and eventually supersede the measurement, reporting and verification system established by decision 1/CP.16, paragraphs 40 to 47 and 60 to 64, and decision 2/CP.17, paragraphs 12 to 62, immediately

following the submission of the final biennial reports and biennial update reports;

GLOBAL STOCKTAKE

100. Requests the Ad Hoc Working Group on the Paris Agreement to identify the sources of input for the global stock-take referred to in Article 14 of the Agreement and to report to the Conference of the Parties, with a view to the Conference of the Parties making a recommendation to the Conference of the Parties serving as the meeting of the Parties to the Paris Agreement for consideration and adoption at its first session, including, but not limited to:

(a) Information on:

(i) The overall effect of the nationally determined contributions communicated by Parties;

(ii) The state of adaptation efforts, support, experiences and priorities from the communications referred to in Article 7, paragraphs 10 and 11, of the Agreement, and reports referred to in Article 13, paragraph 7, of the Agreement;

(iii) The mobilization and provision of support;

(b) The latest reports of the Intergovernmental Panel on Climate Change;

(c) Reports of the subsidiary bodies;

101. Also requests the Subsidiary Body for Scientific and Technological Advice to provide advice on how the assessments of the Intergovernmental Panel on Climate Change can inform the global stock-take of the implementation of the Agreement pursuant to its Article 14 of the Agreement and to report on this matter to the Ad Hoc Working Group on the Paris Agreement at its second session;

102. Further requests the Ad Hoc Working Group on the Paris Agreement to develop modalities for the global stock-take referred to in Article 14 of the Agreement and to report to the

Conference of the Parties, with a view to making a recommendation to the Conference of the Parties serving as the meeting of the Parties to the Paris Agreement for consideration and adoption at its first session;

FACILITATING IMPLEMENTATION AND COMPLIANCE

103. Decides that the committee referred to in Article 15, paragraph 2, of the Agreement shall consist of 12 members with recognized competence in relevant scientific, technical, socio-economic or legal fields, to be elected by the Conference of the Parties serving as the meeting of the Parties to the Paris Agreement on the basis of equitable geographical representation, with two members each from the five regional groups of the United Nations and one member each from the small island developing States and the least developed countries, while taking into account the goal of gender balance;

104. Requests the Ad Hoc Working Group on the Paris Agreement to develop the modalities and procedures for the effective operation of the committee referred to in Article 15, paragraph 2, of the Agreement, with a view to the Ad Hoc Working Group on the Paris Agreement completing its work on such modalities and procedures for consideration and adoption by the Conference of the Parties serving as the meeting of the Parties to the Paris Agreement at its first session;

FINAL CLAUSES

105. Also requests the secretariat, solely for the purposes of Article 21 of the Agreement, to make available on its website on the date of adoption of the Agreement as well as in the report of the Conference of the Parties at its twenty-first session, information on the most up-to-date total and per cent of greenhouse gas emissions

communicated by Parties to the Convention in their national communications, greenhouse gas inventory reports, biennial reports or biennial update reports;

ENHANCED ACTION PRIOR TO 2020

106. Resolves to ensure the highest possible mitigation efforts in the pre-2020 period, including by:

(a) Urging all Parties to the Kyoto Protocol that have not already done so to ratify and implement the Doha Amendment to the Kyoto Protocol;

(b) Urging all Parties that have not already done so to make and implement a mitigation pledge under the Cancun Agreements;

(c) Reiterating its resolve, as set out in decision 1/CP.19, paragraphs 3 and 4, to accelerate the full implementation of the decisions constituting the agreed outcome pursuant to decision 1/CP.13 and enhance ambition in the pre-2020 period in order to ensure the highest possible mitigation efforts under the Convention by all Parties;

(d) Inviting developing country Parties that have not submitted their first biennial update reports to do so as soon as possible;

(e) Urging all Parties to participate in the existing measurement, reporting and verification processes under the Cancun Agreements, in a timely manner, with a view to demonstrating progress made in the implementation of their mitigation pledges;

107. Encourages Parties to promote the voluntary cancellation by Party and non-Party stakeholders, without double counting of units issued under the Kyoto Protocol, including certified emission reductions that are valid for the second commitment period;

108. Urges host and purchasing Parties to report transparently on internationally transferred mitigation outcomes,

including outcomes used to meet international pledges, and emission units issued under the Kyoto Protocol with a view to promoting environmental integrity and avoiding double counting;

109. Recognizes the social, economic and environmental value of voluntary mitigation actions and their co-benefits for adaptation, health and sustainable development;

110. Resolves to strengthen, in the period 2016–2020, the existing technical examination process on mitigation in taking into account the latest scientific knowledge, including by:

(a) Encouraging Parties, Convention bodies and international organizations to engage in this process, including, as appropriate, in cooperation with relevant non-Party stakeholders, to share their experiences and suggestions, including from regional events, and to cooperate in facilitating the implementation of policies, practices and actions identified during this process in accordance with national sustainable development priorities;

(b) Striving to improve, in consultation with Parties, access to and participation in this process by developing country Party and non-Party experts;

(c) Requesting the Technology Executive Committee and the Climate Technology Centre and Network in accordance with their respective mandates:

(i) To engage in the technical expert meetings and enhance their efforts to facilitate and support Parties in scaling up the implementation of policies, practices and actions identified during this process;

(ii) To provide regular updates during the technical expert meetings on the progress made in facilitating the implementation of policies, practices and actions previously identified during this process;

(iii) To include information on their activities under this process in their joint annual report to the Conference of the Parties;

(d) Encouraging Parties to make effective use of the Climate Technology Centre and Network to obtain assistance to develop economically, environmentally and socially viable project proposals in the high mitigation potential areas identified in this process;

111. Encourages the operating entities of the Financial Mechanism of the Convention to engage in the technical expert meetings and to inform participants of their contribution to facilitating progress in the implementation of policies, practices and actions identified during the technical examination process;

112. Requests the secretariat to organize the process referred to in paragraph 110 above and disseminate its results, including by:

(a) Organizing, in consultation with the Technology Executive Committee and relevant expert organizations, regular technical expert meetings focusing on specific policies, practices and actions representing best practices and with the potential to be scalable and replicable;

(b) Updating, on an annual basis and in time to serve as input to the summary for policymakers referred to, a technical paper on the mitigation benefits and co-benefits of policies, practices and actions for enhancing mitigation ambition, as well as on options for supporting their implementation, information on which should be made available in a user-friendly online format;

(c) Preparing, in consultation with the champions referred to a summary for policymakers, with information on specific policies, practices and actions representing best practices and with the potential to be scalable and replicable, and on options to support their implementation, as well as on relevant collaborative initiatives, and publishing the summary at least two months in advance of each session of the Conference of the Parties as input for the high-level

113. Decides that the process referred to should be organized jointly by the Subsidiary Body for Implementation and the Subsidiary Body for Scientific and Technological Advice and

should take place on an ongoing basis until 2020;

114. Also decides to conduct in 2017 an assessment of the process so as to improve its effectiveness;

115. Resolves to enhance the provision of urgent and adequate finance, technology and capacity-building support by developed country Parties in order to enhance the level of ambition of pre-2020 action by Parties, and in this regard strongly urges developed country Parties to scale up their level of financial support, with a concrete roadmap to achieve the goal of jointly providing USD 100 billion annually by 2020 for mitigation and adaptation while significantly increasing adaptation finance from current levels and to further provide appropriate technology and capacity-building support;

116. Decides to conduct a facilitative dialogue in conjunction with the twenty-second session of the Conference of the Parties to assess the progress in implementing decision and identify relevant opportunities to enhance the provision of financial resources, including for technology development and transfer and capacity-building support, with a view to identifying ways to enhance the ambition of mitigation efforts by all Parties, including identifying relevant opportunities to enhance the provision and mobilization of support and enabling environments;

117. Acknowledges with appreciation the results of the Lima-Paris Action Agenda, which build on the climate summit convened on 23 September 2014 by the Secretary-General of the United Nations;

118. Welcomes the efforts of non-Party stakeholders to scale up their climate actions, and encourages the registration of those actions in the Non-State Actor Zone for Climate Action platform.

119. Encourages Parties to work closely with non-Party stakeholders to catalyse efforts to strengthen mitigation and adaptation action;

120. Also encourages non-Party stakeholders to increase their engagement in the processes referred to in paragraph 110 above and paragraph 125 below;

121. Agrees to convene, pursuant to decision building on the Lima-Paris Action Agenda and in conjunction with each session of the Conference of the Parties during the period 2016–2020, a high-level event that:

(a) Further strengthens high-level engagement on the implementation of policy options and actions arising from the processes and drawing on the summary for policymakers.

(b) Provides an opportunity for announcing new or strengthened voluntary efforts, initiatives and coalitions, including the implementation of policies, practices and actions arising from the processes and presented in the summary for policymakers.

(c) Takes stock of related progress and recognizes new or strengthened voluntary efforts, initiatives and coalitions;

(d) Provides meaningful and regular opportunities for the effective high-level engagement of dignitaries of Parties, organizations, international cooperative initiatives and non-Party stakeholders;

122. Decides that two high-level champions shall be appointed to act on behalf of the President of the Conference of the Parties to facilitate through strengthened high-level engagement in the period 2016–2020 the successful execution of existing efforts and the scaling-up and introduction of new or strengthened voluntary efforts, initiatives and coalitions, including by:

(a) Working with the Executive Secretary and the current and incoming Presidents of the Conference of the Parties to coordinate the annual high-level

(b) Engaging with interested Parties and non-Party stakeholders, including to further the voluntary initiatives of the Lima-Paris Action Agenda;

(c) Providing guidance to the secretariat on the organization of technical expert meetings

123. Also decides that the high-level champions referred to in paragraph 122 above should normally serve for a term of two years, with their terms overlapping for a full year to ensure continuity, such that:

(a) The President of the Conference of the Parties of the twenty-first session should appoint one champion, who should serve for one year from the date of the appointment until the last day of the Conference of the Parties at its twenty-second session;

(b) The President of the Conference of the Parties of the twenty-second session should appoint one champion who should serve for two years from the date of the appointment until the last day of the Conference of the Parties at its twenty-third session (November 2017);

(c) Thereafter, each subsequent President of the Conference of the Parties should appoint one champion who should serve for two years and succeed the previously appointed champion whose term has ended;

124. Invites all interested Parties and relevant organizations to provide support for the work of the champions

125. Decides to launch, in the period 2016□2020, a technical examination process on adaptation;

126. Also decides that the technical examination process on adaptation will endeavour to identify concrete opportunities for strengthening resilience, reducing vulnerabilities and increasing the understanding and implementation of adaptation actions;

127. Further decides that the technical examination process should be organized jointly by the Subsidiary Body for Implementation and the Subsidiary Body for Scientific and Technological Advice, and conducted by the Adaptation Committee;

128. Decides that the process will be pursued by:

(a) Facilitating the sharing of good practices, experiences and lessons learned;
(b) Identifying actions that could significantly enhance the implementation of adaptation actions, including actions that could enhance economic diversification and have mitigation co-benefits;
(c) Promoting cooperative action on adaptation;
(d) Identifying opportunities to strengthen enabling environments and enhance the provision of support for adaptation in the context of specific policies, practices and actions;

129. Also decides that the technical examination process on adaptation will take into account the process, modalities, outputs, outcomes and lessons learned from the technical examination process on mitigation

130. Requests the secretariat to support the technical examination process by:

(a) Organizing regular technical expert meetings focusing on specific policies, strategies and actions;
(b) Preparing annually, on the basis of the meetings and in time to serve as an input to the summary for policymakers referred to a technical paper on opportunities to enhance adaptation action, as well as options to support their implementation, information on which should be made available in a user-friendly online format;

131. Decides that in conducting the process the Adaptation Committee will engage with and explore ways to take into account,

synergize with and build on the existing arrangements for the existing arrangements for adaptation-related work programmes, bodies and institutions under the Convention so as to ensure coherence and maximum value;

132. Also decides to conduct, in conjunction with an assessment of the process, so as to improve its effectiveness;

133. Invites Parties and observer organizations to submit information on the opportunities by 3 February 2016;

NON-PARTY STAKEHOLDERS

134. Welcomes the efforts of all non-Party stakeholders to address and respond to climate change, including those of civil society, the private sector, financial institutions, cities and other subnational authorities;

135. Invites the non-Party stakeholders to scale up their efforts and support actions to reduce emissions and/or to build resilience and decrease vulnerability to the adverse effects of climate change and demonstrate these efforts via the Non-State Actor Zone for Climate Action platform.

136. Recognizes the need to strengthen knowledge, technologies, practices and efforts of local communities and indigenous peoples related to addressing and responding to climate change, and establishes a platform for the exchange of experiences and sharing of best practices on mitigation and adaptation in a holistic and integrated manner;

137. Also recognizes the important role of providing incentives for emission reduction activities, including tools such as domestic policies and carbon pricing;

ADMINISTRATIVE AND BUDGETARY MATTERS

138. Takes note of the estimated budgetary implications of the activities to be undertaken by the secretariat referred to in this decision and requests that the actions of the secretariat called for in this decision be undertaken subject to the availability of financial resources;

139. Emphasizes the urgency of making additional resources available for the implementation of the relevant actions, including actions referred to in this decision, and the implementation of the work programme

140. Urges Parties to make voluntary contributions for the timely implementation of this decision.

PARIS AGREEMENT

The Parties to this Agreement, Being Parties to the United Nations Framework Convention on Climate Change, hereinafter referred to as "the Convention",

Pursuant to the Durban Platform for Enhanced Action established by decision 1/CP.17 of the Conference of the Parties to the Convention at its seventeenth session,

In pursuit of the objective of the Convention, and being guided by its principles, including the principle of equity and common but differentiated responsibilities and respective capabilities, in the light of different national circumstances,

Recognizing the need for an effective and progressive response to the urgent threat of climate change on the basis of the best available scientific knowledge,

Also recognizing the specific needs and special circumstances of developing country Parties, especially those that are particularly vulnerable to the adverse effects of climate change, as provided for in the Convention,

Taking full account of the specific needs and special situations of the least developed countries with regard to funding and transfer of technology,

Recognizing that Parties may be affected not only by climate change, but also by the impacts of the measures taken in response to it,

Emphasizing the intrinsic relationship that climate change actions, responses and impacts have with equitable access to sustainable development and eradication of poverty,

Recognizing the fundamental priority of safeguarding food security and ending hunger, and the particular vulnerabilities of food production systems to the adverse impacts of climate change,

Taking into account the imperatives of a just transition of the workforce and the creation of decent work and quality jobs in accordance with nationally defined development priorities,

Acknowledging that climate change is a common concern of humankind, Parties should, when taking action to address climate change, respect, promote and consider their respective obligations on human rights, the right to health, the rights of indigenous peoples, local communities, migrants, children, persons with disabilities and people in vulnerable situations and the right to development, as well as gender equality, empowerment of women and intergenerational equity,

Recognizing the importance of the conservation and enhancement, as appropriate, of sinks and reservoirs of the greenhouse gases referred to in the Convention,

Noting the importance of ensuring the integrity of all ecosystems, including oceans, and the protection of biodiversity, recognized by some cultures as Mother Earth, and noting the importance for some of the concept of "climate justice", when taking action to address climate change,

Affirming the importance of education, training, public awareness, public participation, public access to information and cooperation at all levels on the matters addressed in this Agreement,

Recognizing the importance of the engagements of all levels of government and various actors, in accordance with respective national legislations of Parties, in addressing climate change,

Also recognizing that sustainable lifestyles and sustainable patterns of consumption and production, with developed country Parties taking the lead, play an important role in addressing climate change, have agreed as follows:

For the purpose of this Agreement, the definitions contained in Article 1 of the Convention shall apply. In addition:

1. "Convention" means the United Nations Framework Convention on Climate Change, adopted in New York on 9 May 1992.

2. "Conference of the Parties" means the Conference of the Parties to the Convention.

3. "Party" means a Party to this Agreement.

Article 2

1. This Agreement, in enhancing the implementation of the Convention, including its objective, aims to strengthen the global response to the threat of climate change, in the context of sustainable development and efforts to eradicate poverty, including by:

(a) Holding the increase in the global average temperature to well below 2 °C above pre-industrial levels and to pursue efforts to limit the temperature increase to 1.5 °C above pre-industrial levels, recognizing that this would significantly reduce the risks and impacts of climate change;

(b) Increasing the ability to adapt to the adverse impacts of climate change and foster climate resilience and low greenhouse gas emissions development, in a manner that does not threaten food production;

(c) Making finance flows consistent with a pathway towards low greenhouse gas emissions and climate-resilient development.

2. This Agreement will be implemented to reflect equity and the principle of common but differentiated responsibilities and respective capabilities, in the light of different national circumstances.

Article 3

As nationally determined contributions to the global response to climate change, all Parties are to undertake and communicate ambitious efforts as defined in Articles 4, 7, 9, 10, 11 and 13 with the view to achieving the purpose of this Agreement as set out in Article 2. The efforts of all Parties will represent a progression over time, while recognizing the need to support developing country Parties for the effective implementation of this Agreement.

Article 4

1. In order to achieve the long-term temperature goal set out in Article 2, Parties aim to reach global peaking of greenhouse gas emissions as soon as possible, recognizing that peaking will take longer for developing country Parties, and to undertake rapid reductions thereafter in accordance with best available science, so as to achieve a balance between anthropogenic emissions by sources and removals by sinks of greenhouse gases in the second half of this century, on the basis of equity, and in the context of sustainable development and efforts to eradicate poverty.

2. Each Party shall prepare, communicate and maintain successive nationally determined contributions that it intends to achieve. Parties shall pursue domestic mitigation measures, with the aim of achieving the objectives of such contributions.

3. Each Party's successive nationally determined contribution will represent a progression beyond the Party's then current nationally determined contribution and reflect its highest possible ambition, reflecting its common but differentiated responsibilities and respective capabilities, in the light of different national circumstances.

4. Developed country Parties should continue taking the lead by undertaking economy-wide absolute emission reduction targets. Developing country Parties should continue enhancing their mitigation efforts, and are encouraged to move over time towards economy-wide emission reduction or limitation targets in the light of different national circumstances.

5. Support shall be provided to developing country Parties for the implementation of this Article, in accordance with Articles 9, 10 and 11, recognizing that enhanced support for developing country Parties will allow for higher ambition in their actions.

6. The least developed countries and small island developing States may prepare and communicate strategies, plans and actions for low greenhouse gas emissions development reflecting their special circumstances.

7. Mitigation co-benefits resulting from Parties' adaptation actions and/or economic diversification plans can contribute to mitigation outcomes under this Article.

8. In communicating their nationally determined contributions, all Parties shall provide the information necessary for \ clarity, transparency and understanding in accordance with decision 1/CP.21 and any relevant decisions of the Conference of the Parties serving as the meeting of the Parties to the Paris Agreement.

9. Each Party shall communicate a nationally determined

contribution every five years in accordance with decision 1/CP.21 and any relevant decisions of the Conference of the Parties serving as the meeting of the Parties to the Paris Agreement and be informed by the outcomes of the global stock-take referred to in Article 14.

10. The Conference of the Parties serving as the meeting of the Parties to the Paris Agreement shall consider common time frames for nationally determined contributions at its first session.

11. A Party may at any time adjust its existing nationally determined contribution with a view to enhancing its level of ambition, in accordance with guidance adopted by the Conference of the Parties serving as the meeting of the Parties to the Paris Agreement.

12. Nationally determined contributions communicated by Parties shall be recorded in a public registry maintained by the secretariat.

13. Parties shall account for their nationally determined contributions. In accounting for anthropogenic emissions and removals corresponding to their nationally determined contributions, Parties shall promote environmental integrity, transparency, accuracy, completeness, comparability and consistency, and ensure the avoidance of double counting, in accordance with guidance adopted by the Conference of the Parties serving as the meeting of the Parties to the Paris Agreement.

14. In the context of their nationally determined contributions, when recognizing and implementing mitigation actions with respect to anthropogenic emissions and removals, Parties should take into account, as appropriate, existing methods and guidance under the Convention, in the light of the provisions of paragraph 13 of this Article.

15. Parties shall take into consideration in the implementation of this Agreement the concerns of Parties with economies most affected by the impacts of response measures, particularly developing country Parties.

16. Parties, including regional economic integration organizations and their member States, that have reached an agreement to act jointly under paragraph 2 of this Article shall notify the secretariat of the terms of that agreement, including the emission level allocated to each Party within the relevant time period, when they communicate their nationally determined contributions. The secretariat shall in turn inform the Parties and signatories to the Convention of the terms of that agreement.

17. Each party to such an agreement shall be responsible for its emission level as set out in the agreement referred to in paragraph 16 above in accordance with paragraphs 13 and 14 of this Article and Articles 13 and 15.

18. If Parties acting jointly do so in the framework of, and together with, a regional economic integration organization which is itself a Party to this Agreement, each member State of that regional economic integration organization individually, and together with the regional economic integration organization, shall be responsible for its emission level as set out in the agreement communicated under paragraph 16 of this Article in accordance with paragraphs 13 and 14 of this Article and Articles 13 and 15.

19. All Parties should strive to formulate and communicate long-term low greenhouse gas emission development strategies, mindful of Article 2 taking into account their common but differentiated responsibilities and respective capabilities, in the light of different national circumstances.

Article 5

1. Parties should take action to conserve and enhance, as appropriate, sinks and reservoirs of greenhouse gases as referred to in Article 4, paragraph 1(d), of the Convention, including forests.

2. Parties are encouraged to take action to implement and support, including through results-based payments, the existing framework as set out in related guidance and decisions already agreed under the Convention for: policy approaches and positive incentives for activities relating to reducing emissions from deforestation and forest degradation, and the role of conservation, sustainable management of forests and enhancement of forest carbon stocks in developing countries; and alternative policy approaches, such as joint mitigation and adaptation approaches for the integral and sustainable management of forests, while reaffirming the importance of incentivizing, as appropriate, non-carbon benefits associated with such approaches.

Article 6

1. Parties recognize that some Parties choose to pursue voluntary cooperation in the implementation of their nationally determined contributions to allow for higher ambition in their mitigation and adaptation actions and to promote sustainable development and environmental integrity.

2. Parties shall, where engaging on a voluntary basis in cooperative approaches that involve the use of internationally transferred mitigation outcomes towards nationally determined contributions, promote sustainable development and ensure environmental integrity and transparency, including in governance, and shall apply robust accounting to ensure, inter alia, the avoidance of double counting, consistent with guidance adopted by the Conference of the Parties serving as the meeting of the Parties to the

Paris Agreement.

3. The use of internationally transferred mitigation outcomes to achieve nationally determined contributions under this Agreement shall be voluntary and authorized by participating Parties.

4. A mechanism to contribute to the mitigation of greenhouse gas emissions and support sustainable development is hereby established under the authority and guidance of the Conference of the Parties serving as the meeting of the Parties to the Paris Agreement for use by Parties on a voluntary basis. It shall be supervised by a body designated by the Conference of the Parties serving as the meeting of the Parties to the Paris Agreement, and shall aim:

(a) To promote the mitigation of greenhouse gas emissions while fostering sustainable development;

(b) To incentivize and facilitate participation in the mitigation of greenhouse gas emissions by public and private entities authorized by a Party;

(c) To contribute to the reduction of emission levels in the host Party, which will benefit from mitigation activities resulting in emission reductions that can also be used by another Party to fulfil its nationally determined contribution; and

(d) To deliver an overall mitigation in global emissions.

5. Emission reductions resulting from the mechanism referred to in paragraph 4 of this Article shall not be used to demonstrate achievement of the host Party's nationally determined contribution if used by another Party to demonstrate achievement of its nationally determined contribution.

6. The Conference of the Parties serving as the meeting of the Parties to the Paris Agreement shall ensure that a share of the proceeds from activities under the mechanism referred to in paragraph 4 of this Article is used to cover administrative expenses

as well as to assist developing country Parties that are particularly vulnerable to the adverse effects of climate change to meet the costs of adaptation.

7. The Conference of the Parties serving as the meeting of the Parties to the Paris Agreement shall adopt rules, modalities and procedures for the mechanism referred to in paragraph 4 of this Article at its first session.

8. Parties recognize the importance of integrated, holistic and balanced non-market approaches being available to Parties to assist in the implementation of their nationally determined contributions, in the context of sustainable development and poverty eradication, in a coordinated and effective manner, including through, inter alia, mitigation, adaptation, finance, technology transfer and capacity-building, as appropriate. These approaches shall aim to:
(a) Promote mitigation and adaptation ambition;
(b) Enhance public and private sector participation in the implementation of nationally determined contributions; and
(c) Enable opportunities for coordination across instruments and relevant institutional arrangements.

9. A framework for non-market approaches to sustainable development is hereby defined to promote the non-market approaches referred to in paragraph 8 of this Article.

Article 7

1. Parties hereby establish the global goal on adaptation of enhancing adaptive capacity, strengthening resilience and reducing vulnerability to climate change, with a view to contributing to sustainable development and ensuring an adequate adaptation response in the context of the temperature goal referred to in Article

2. Parties recognize that adaptation is a global challenge

faced by all with local, subnational, national, regional and international dimensions, and that it is a key component of and makes a contribution to the long-term global response to climate change to protect people, livelihoods and ecosystems, taking into account the urgent and immediate needs of those developing country Parties that are particularly vulnerable to the adverse effects of climate change.

3. The adaptation efforts of developing country Parties shall be recognized, in accordance with the modalities to be adopted by the Conference of the Parties serving as the meeting of the Parties to the Paris Agreement at its first session.

4. Parties recognize that the current need for adaptation is significant and that greater levels of mitigation can reduce the need for additional adaptation efforts, and that greater adaptation needs can involve greater adaptation costs.

5. Parties acknowledge that adaptation action should follow a country-driven, gender-responsive, participatory and fully transparent approach, taking into consideration vulnerable groups, communities and ecosystems, and should be based on and guided by the best available science and, as appropriate, traditional knowledge, knowledge of indigenous peoples and local knowledge systems, with a view to integrating adaptation into relevant socioeconomic and environmental policies and actions, where appropriate.

6. Parties recognize the importance of support for and international cooperation on adaptation efforts and the importance of taking into account the needs of developing country Parties, especially those that are particularly vulnerable to the adverse effects of climate change.

7. Parties should strengthen their cooperation on enhancing action on adaptation, taking into account the Cancun Adaptation

Framework, including with regard to:

(a) Sharing information, good practices, experiences and lessons learned, including, as appropriate, as these relate to science, planning, policies and implementation in relation to adaptation actions;

(b) Strengthening institutional arrangements, including those under the Convention that serve this Agreement, to support the synthesis of relevant information and knowledge, and the provision of technical support and guidance to Parties;

(c) Strengthening scientific knowledge on climate, including research, systematic observation of the climate system and early warning systems, in a manner that informs climate services and supports decision-making;

(d) Assisting developing country Parties in identifying effective adaptation practices, adaptation needs, priorities, support provided and received for adaptation actions and efforts, and challenges and gaps, in a manner consistent with encouraging good practices;

(e) Improving the effectiveness and durability of adaptation actions.

8. United Nations specialized organizations and agencies are encouraged to support the efforts of Parties to implement the actions referred to in paragraph 7 of this Article, taking into account the provisions of paragraph 5 of this Article.

9. Each Party shall, as appropriate, engage in adaptation planning processes and the implementation of actions, including the development or enhancement of relevant plans, policies and/or contributions, which may include:

(a) The implementation of adaptation actions, undertakings and/or efforts;

(b) The process to formulate and implement national adaptation plans;

(c) The assessment of climate change impacts and vulnerability, with a view to formulating nationally determined prioritized actions, taking into account vulnerable people, places and ecosystems;

(d) Monitoring and evaluating and learning from adaptation plans, policies, programmes and actions; and

(e) Building the resilience of socioeconomic and ecological systems, including through economic diversification and sustainable management of natural resources.

10. Each Party should, as appropriate, submit and update periodically an adaptation communication, which may include its priorities, implementation and support needs, plans and actions, without creating any additional burden for developing country Parties.

11. The adaptation communication referred to in paragraph 10 of this Article shall be, as appropriate, submitted and updated periodically, as a component of or in conjunction with other communications or documents, including a national adaptation plan, a nationally determined contribution as referred to in Article 4, paragraph 2, and/or a national communication.

12. The adaptation communications referred to in paragraph 10 of this Article shall be recorded in a public registry maintained by the secretariat.

13. Continuous and enhanced international support shall be provided to developing country Parties for the implementation of paragraphs 7, 9, 10 and 11 of this Article, in accordance with the provisions of Articles 9, 10 and 11.

14. The global stock-take referred to in Article 14 shall, inter alia:

(a) Recognize adaptation efforts of developing country Parties;

(b) Enhance the implementation of adaptation action taking into account the adaptation communication referred to in paragraph 10 of this Article;

(c) Review the adequacy and effectiveness of adaptation and support provided for adaptation; and

(d) Review the overall progress made in achieving the global goal on adaptation referred to in paragraph 1 of this Article.

Article 8

1. Parties recognize the importance of averting, minimizing and addressing loss and damage associated with the adverse effects of climate change, including extreme weather events and slow onset events, and the role of sustainable development in reducing the risk of loss and damage.

2. The Warsaw International Mechanism for Loss and Damage associated with Climate Change Impacts shall be subject to the authority and guidance of the Conference of the Parties serving as the meeting of the Parties to the Paris Agreement and may be enhanced and strengthened, as determined by the Conference of the Parties serving as the meeting of the Parties to the Paris Agreement.

3. Parties should enhance understanding, action and support, including through the Warsaw International Mechanism, as appropriate, on a cooperative and facilitative basis with respect to loss and damage associated with the adverse effects of climate change.

4. Accordingly, areas of cooperation and facilitation to enhance understanding, action and support may include:
(a) Early warning systems;
(b) Emergency preparedness;
(c) Slow onset events;

(d) Events that may involve irreversible and permanent loss and damage;

(e) Comprehensive risk assessment and management;

(f) Risk insurance facilities, climate risk pooling and other insurance solutions;

(g) Non-economic losses;

(h) Resilience of communities, livelihoods and ecosystems.

5. The Warsaw International Mechanism shall collaborate with existing bodies and expert groups under the Agreement, as well as relevant organizations and expert bodies outside the Agreement.

Article 9

1. Developed country Parties shall provide financial resources to assist developing country Parties with respect to both mitigation and adaptation in continuation of their existing obligations under the Convention.

2. Other Parties are encouraged to provide or continue to provide such support voluntarily.

3. As part of a global effort, developed country Parties should continue to take the lead in mobilizing climate finance from a wide variety of sources, instruments and channels, noting the significant role of public funds, through a variety of actions, including supporting country-driven strategies, and taking into account the needs and priorities of developing country Parties. Such mobilization of climate finance should represent a progression beyond previous efforts.

4. The provision of scaled-up financial resources should aim to achieve a balance between adaptation and mitigation, taking into account country-driven strategies, and the priorities and needs of developing country Parties, especially those that are particularly

vulnerable to the adverse effects of climate change and have significant capacity constraints, such as the least developed countries and small island developing States, considering the need for public and grant-based resources for adaptation.

5. Developed country Parties shall biennially communicate indicative quantitative and qualitative information related to paragraphs 1 and 3 of this Article, as applicable, including, as available, projected levels of public financial resources to be provided to developing country Parties. Other Parties providing resources are encouraged to communicate biennially such information on a voluntary basis.

6. The global stock-take referred to in Article 14 shall take into account the relevant information provided by developed country Parties and/or Agreement bodies on efforts related to climate finance.

7. Developed country Parties shall provide transparent and consistent information on support for developing country Parties provided and mobilized through public interventions biennially in accordance with the modalities, procedures and guidelines to be adopted by the Conference of the Parties serving as the meeting of the Parties to the Paris Agreement, at its first session, as stipulated in Article 13, paragraph 13. Other Parties are encouraged to do so.

8. The Financial Mechanism of the Convention, including its operating entities, shall serve as the financial mechanism of this Agreement.

9. The institutions serving this Agreement, including the operating entities of the Financial Mechanism of the Convention, shall aim to ensure efficient access to financial resources through simplified approval procedures and enhanced readiness support for developing country Parties, in particular for the least developed

countries and small island developing States, in the context of their national climate strategies and plans

Article 10

1. Parties share a long-term vision on the importance of fully realizing technology development and transfer in order to improve resilience to climate change and to reduce greenhouse gas emissions.

2. Parties, noting the importance of technology for the implementation of mitigation and adaptation actions under this Agreement and recognizing existing technology deployment and dissemination efforts, shall strengthen cooperative action on technology development and transfer.

3. The Technology Mechanism established under the Convention shall serve this Agreement.

4. A technology framework is hereby established to provide overarching guidance to the work of the Technology Mechanism in promoting and facilitating enhanced action on technology development and transfer in order to support the implementation of this Agreement, in pursuit of the long-term vision referred to in paragraph 1 of this Article.

5. Accelerating, encouraging and enabling innovation is critical for an effective, long-term global response to climate change and promoting economic growth and sustainable development. Such effort shall be, as appropriate, supported, including by the Technology Mechanism and, through financial means, by the Financial Mechanism of the Convention, for collaborative approaches to research and development, and facilitating access to technology, in particular for early stages of the technology cycle, to developing country Parties.

6. Support, including financial support, shall be provided to developing country Parties for the implementation of this Article, including for strengthening cooperative action on technology development and transfer at different stages of the technology cycle, with a view to achieving a balance between support for mitigation and adaptation. The global stock-take referred to in Article 14 shall take into account available information on efforts related to support on technology development and transfer for developing country Parties.

Article 11

1. Capacity-building under this Agreement should enhance the capacity and ability of developing country Parties, in particular countries with the least capacity, such as the least developed countries, and those that are particularly vulnerable to the adverse effects of climate change, such as small island developing States, to take effective climate change action, including, inter alia, to implement adaptation and mitigation actions, and should facilitate technology development, dissemination and deployment, access to climate finance, relevant aspects of education, training and public awareness, and the transparent, timely and accurate communication of information.

2. Capacity-building should be country-driven, based on and responsive to national needs, and foster country ownership of Parties, in particular, for developing country Parties, including at the national, subnational and local levels. Capacity-building should be guided by lessons learned, including those from capacity-building activities under the Convention, and should be an effective, iterative process that is participatory, cross-cutting and gender-responsive.

3. All Parties should cooperate to enhance the capacity of developing country Parties to implement this Agreement. Developed country Parties should enhance support for capacity-building actions in developing country Parties.

4. All Parties enhancing the capacity of developing country Parties to implement this Agreement, including through regional, bilateral and multilateral approaches, shall regularly communicate on these actions or measures on capacity-building. Developing country Parties should regularly communicate progress made on implementing capacity-building plans, policies, actions or measures to implement this Agreement.

5. Capacity-building activities shall be enhanced through appropriate institutional arrangements to support the implementation of this Agreement, including the appropriate institutional arrangements established under the Convention that serve this Agreement. The Conference of the Parties serving as the meeting of the Parties to the Paris Agreement shall, at its first session, consider and adopt a decision on the initial institutional arrangements for capacity-building.

Article 12

Parties shall cooperate in taking measures, as appropriate, to enhance climate change education, training, public awareness, public participation and public access to information, recognizing the importance of these steps with respect to enhancing actions under this Agreement.

Article 13

1. In order to build mutual trust and confidence and to promote effective implementation, an enhanced transparency framework for action and support, with built-in flexibility which takes into account Parties' different capacities and builds upon collective experience is hereby established.

2. The transparency framework shall provide flexibility in the

implementation of the provisions of this Article to those developing country Parties that need it in the light of their capacities. The modalities, procedures and guidelines referred to in paragraph 13 of this Article shall reflect such flexibility.

3. The transparency framework shall build on and enhance the transparency arrangements under the Convention, recognizing the special circumstances of the least developed countries and small island developing States, and be implemented in a facilitative, non-intrusive, non-punitive manner, respectful of national sovereignty, and avoid placing undue burden on Parties.

4. The transparency arrangements under the Convention, including national communications, biennial reports and biennial update reports, international assessment and review and international consultation and analysis, shall form part of the experience drawn upon for the development of the modalities, procedures and guidelines under paragraph 13 of this Article.

5. The purpose of the framework for transparency of action is to provide a clear understanding of climate change action in the light of the objective of the Convention as set out in its Article 2, including clarity and tracking of progress towards achieving Parties' individual nationally determined contributions under Article 4, and Parties' adaptation actions under Article 7, including good practices, priorities, needs and gaps, to inform the global stock-take under

Article 14.

6. The purpose of the framework for transparency of support is to provide clarity on support provided and received by relevant individual Parties in the context of climate change actions under Articles 4, 7, 9, 10 and 11, and, to the extent possible, to provide a full overview of aggregate financial support provided, to inform the global stock-take under Article 14.

7. Each Party shall regularly provide the following information:

(a) A national inventory report of anthropogenic emissions by sources and removals by sinks of greenhouse gases, prepared using good practice methodologies accepted by the Intergovernmental Panel on Climate Change and agreed upon by the Conference of the Parties serving as the meeting of the Parties to the Paris Agreement;

(b) Information necessary to track progress made in implementing and achieving its nationally determined contribution under Article 4.

8. Each Party should also provide information related to climate change impacts and adaptation under Article 7, as appropriate.

9. Developed country Parties shall, and other Parties that provide support should, provide information on financial, technology transfer and capacity-building support provided to developing country Parties under Article 9, 10 and 11.

10. Developing country Parties should provide information on financial, technology transfer and capacity-building support needed and received under Articles 9, 10 and 11.

11. Information submitted by each Party under paragraphs 7 and 9 of this Article shall undergo a technical expert review, in accordance with decision 1/CP.21. For those developing country Parties that need it in the light of their capacities, the review process shall include assistance in identifying capacity-building needs. In addition, each Party shall participate in a facilitative, multilateral consideration of progress with respect to efforts under Article 9, and

its respective implementation and achievement of its nationally determined contribution.

12. The technical expert review under this paragraph shall consist of a consideration of the Party's support provided, as relevant, and its implementation and achievement of its nationally determined contribution. The review shall also identify areas of improvement for the Party, and include a review of the consistency of the information with the modalities, procedures and guidelines referred to in paragraph 13 of this Article, taking into account the flexibility accorded to the Party under paragraph 2 of this Article. The review shall pay particular attention to the respective national capabilities and circumstances of developing country Parties.

13. The Conference of the Parties serving as the meeting of the Parties to the Paris Agreement shall, at its first session, building on experience from the arrangements related to transparency under the Convention, and elaborating on the provisions in this Article, adopt common modalities, procedures and guidelines, as appropriate, for the transparency of action and support.

14. Support shall be provided to developing countries for the implementation of this Article.

15. Support shall also be provided for the building of transparency-related capacity of developing country Parties on a continuous basis.

Article 14

1. The Conference of the Parties serving as the meeting of the Parties to the Paris Agreement shall periodically take stock of the implementation of this Agreement to assess the collective progress towards achieving the purpose of this Agreement and its long-term goals (referred to as the "global stock-take"). It shall do so in a

comprehensive and facilitative manner, considering mitigation, adaptation and the means of implementation and support, and in the light of equity and the best available science.

2. The Conference of the Parties serving as the meeting of the Parties to the Paris Agreement shall undertake its first global stock-take in 2023 and every five years thereafter unless otherwise decided by the Conference of the Parties serving as the meeting of the Parties to the Paris Agreement.

3. The outcome of the global stock-take shall inform Parties in updating and enhancing, in a nationally determined manner, their actions and support in accordance with the relevant provisions of this Agreement, as well as in enhancing international cooperation for climate action.

Article 15

1. A mechanism to facilitate implementation of and promote compliance with the provisions of this Agreement is hereby established.

2. The mechanism referred to in paragraph 1 of this Article shall consist of a committee that shall be expert-based and facilitative in nature and function in a manner that is transparent, non-adversarial and non-punitive. The committee shall pay particular attention to the respective national capabilities and circumstances of Parties.

3. The committee shall operate under the modalities and procedures adopted by the Conference of the Parties serving as the meeting of the Parties to the Paris Agreement at its first session and report annually to the Conference of the Parties serving as the meeting of the Parties to the Paris Agreement.

Article 16

1. The Conference of the Parties, the supreme body of the Convention, shall serve as the meeting of the Parties to this Agreement.

2. Parties to the Convention that are not Parties to this Agreement may participate as observers in the proceedings of any session of the Conference of the Parties serving as the meeting of the Parties to this Agreement. When the Conference of the Parties serves as the meeting of the Parties to this Agreement, decisions under this Agreement shall be taken only by those that are Parties to this Agreement.

3. When the Conference of the Parties serves as the meeting of the Parties to this Agreement, any member of the Bureau of the Conference of the Parties representing a Party to the Convention but, at that time, not a Party to this Agreement, shall be replaced by an additional member to be elected by and from amongst the Parties to this Agreement.

4. The Conference of the Parties serving as the meeting of the Parties to the Paris Agreement shall keep under regular review the implementation of this Agreement and shall make, within its mandate, the decisions necessary to promote its effective implementation. It shall perform the functions assigned to it by this Agreement and shall:
(a) Establish such subsidiary bodies as deemed necessary for the implementation of this Agreement; and
(b) Exercise such other functions as may be required for the implementation of this Agreement.

5. The rules of procedure of the Conference of the Parties and the financial procedures applied under the Convention shall be applied mutatis mutandis under this Agreement, except as may be

otherwise decided by consensus by the Conference of the Parties serving as the meeting of the Parties to the Paris Agreement.

6. The first session of the Conference of the Parties serving as the meeting of the Parties to the Paris Agreement shall be convened by the secretariat in conjunction with the first session of the Conference of the Parties that is scheduled after the date of entry into force of this Agreement. Subsequent ordinary sessions of the Conference of the Parties serving as the meeting of the Parties to the Paris Agreement shall be held in conjunction with ordinary sessions of the Conference of the Parties, unless otherwise decided by the Conference of the Parties serving as the meeting of the Parties to the Paris Agreement.

7. Extraordinary sessions of the Conference of the Parties serving as the meeting of the Parties to the Paris Agreement shall be held at such other times as may be deemed necessary by the Conference of the Parties serving as the meeting of the Parties to the Paris Agreement or at the written request of any Party, provided that, within six months of the request being communicated to the Parties by the secretariat, it is supported by at least one third of the Parties.

8. The United Nations and its specialized agencies and the International Atomic Energy Agency, as well as any State member thereof or observers thereto not party to the Convention, may be represented at sessions of the Conference of the Parties serving as the meeting of the Parties to the Paris Agreement as observers. Anybody or agency, whether national or international, governmental or non-governmental, which is qualified in matters covered by this Agreement and which has informed the secretariat of its wish to be represented at a session of the Conference of the Parties serving as the meeting of the Parties to the Paris Agreement as an observer, may be so admitted unless at least one third of the Parties present object. The admission and participation of observers shall be subject to the rules of procedure referred to in paragraph 5 of this Article.

Article 17

1. The secretariat established by Article 8 of the Convention shall serve as the secretariat of this Agreement.

2. Article 8, paragraph 2, of the Convention on the functions of the secretariat, and Article 8, paragraph 3, of the Convention, on the arrangements made for the functioning of the secretariat, shall apply mutatis mutandis to this Agreement. The secretariat shall, in addition, exercise the functions assigned to it under this Agreement and by the Conference of the Parties serving as the meeting of the Parties to the Paris Agreement.

Article 18

1. The Subsidiary Body for Scientific and Technological Advice and the Subsidiary Body for Implementation established by Articles 9 and 10 of the Convention shall serve, respectively, as the Subsidiary Body for Scientific and Technological Advice and the Subsidiary Body for Implementation of this Agreement. The provisions of the Convention relating to the functioning of these two bodies shall apply mutatis mutandis to this Agreement. Sessions of the meetings of the Subsidiary Body for Scientific and Technological Advice and the Subsidiary Body for Implementation of this Agreement shall be held in conjunction with the meetings of, respectively, the Subsidiary Body for Scientific and Technological Advice and the Subsidiary Body for Implementation of the Convention.

2. Parties to the Convention that are not Parties to this Agreement may participate as observers in the proceedings of any session of the subsidiary bodies. When the subsidiary bodies serve as the subsidiary bodies of this Agreement, decisions under this Agreement shall be taken only by those that are Parties to this

Agreement.

3. When the subsidiary bodies established by Articles 9 and 10 of the Convention exercise their functions with regard to matters concerning this Agreement, any member of the bureaux of those subsidiary bodies representing a Party to the Convention but, at that time, not a Party to this Agreement, shall be replaced by an additional member to be elected by and from amongst the Parties to this Agreement.

Article 19

1. Subsidiary bodies or other institutional arrangements established by or under the Convention, other than those referred to in this Agreement, shall serve this Agreement upon a decision of the Conference of the Parties serving as the meeting of the Parties to the Paris Agreement. The Conference of the Parties serving as the meeting of the Parties to the Paris Agreement shall specify the functions to be exercised by such subsidiary bodies or arrangements.

2. The Conference of the Parties serving as the meeting of the Parties to the Paris Agreement may provide further guidance to such subsidiary bodies and institutional arrangements.

Article 20

1. This Agreement shall be open for signature and subject to ratification, acceptance or approval by States and regional economic integration organizations that are Parties to the Convention. It shall be open for signature at the United Nations Headquarters in New York from 22 April 2016 to 21 April 2017. Thereafter, this Agreement shall be open for accession from the day following the date on which it is closed for signature. Instruments of ratification, acceptance, approval or accession shall be deposited with the Depositary.

2. Any regional economic integration organization that becomes a Party to this Agreement without any of its member States being a Party shall be bound by all the obligations under this Agreement. In the case of regional economic integration organizations with one or more member States that are Parties to this Agreement, the organization and its member States shall decide on their respective responsibilities for the performance of their obligations under this Agreement. In such cases, the organization and the member States shall not be entitled to exercise rights under this Agreement concurrently.

3. In their instruments of ratification, acceptance, approval or accession, regional economic integration organizations shall declare the extent of their competence with respect to the matters governed by this Agreement. These organizations shall also inform the Depositary, who shall in turn inform the Parties, of any substantial modification in the extent of their competence.

Article 21

1. This Agreement shall enter into force on the thirtieth day after the date on which at least 55 Parties to the Convention accounting in total for at least an estimated 55 percent of the total global greenhouse gas emissions have deposited their instruments of ratification, acceptance, approval or accession.

2. Solely for the limited purpose of paragraph 1 of this Article, "total global greenhouse gas emissions" means the most up-to-date amount communicated on or before the date of adoption of this Agreement by the Parties to the Convention.

3. For each State or regional economic integration organization that ratifies, accepts or approves this Agreement or accedes thereto after the conditions set out in paragraph 1 of this

Article for entry into force have been fulfilled, this Agreement shall enter into force on the thirtieth day after the date of deposit by such State or regional economic integration organization of its instrument of ratification, acceptance, approval or accession.

4. For the purposes of paragraph 1 of this Article, any instrument deposited by a regional economic integration organization shall not be counted as additional to those deposited by its member States.

Article 22

The provisions of Article 15 of the Convention on the adoption of amendments to the Convention shall apply mutatis mutandis to this Agreement.

Article 23

1. The provisions of Article 16 of the Convention on the adoption and amendment of annexes to the Convention shall apply mutatis mutandis to this Agreement.

2. Annexes to this Agreement shall form an integral part thereof and, unless otherwise expressly provided for, a reference to this Agreement constitutes at the same time a reference to any annexes thereto. Such annexes shall be restricted to lists, forms and any other material of a descriptive nature that is of a scientific, technical, procedural or administrative character.

Article 24

The provisions of Article 14 of the Convention on settlement of disputes shall apply mutatis mutandis to this Agreement.

Article 25

1. Each Party shall have one vote, except as provided for paragraph 2 of this Article.

2. Regional economic integration organizations, in matters within their competence, shall exercise their right to vote with a number of votes equal to the number of their member States that are Parties to this Agreement. Such an organization shall not exercise its right to vote if any of its member States exercises its right, and vice versa.

Article 26

The Secretary-General of the United Nations shall be the Depositary of this Agreement.

Article 27

No reservations may be made to this Agreement.

Article 28

1. At any time after three years from the date on which this Agreement has entered into force for a Party that Party may withdraw from this Agreement by giving written notification to the Depositary.

2. Any such withdrawal shall take effect upon expiry of one year from the date of receipt by the Depositary of the notification of withdrawal, or on such later date as may be specified in the notification of withdrawal.

3. Any Party that withdraws from the Convention shall be considered as also having withdrawn from this Agreement.

Article 29

The original of this Agreement, of which the Arabic, Chinese, English, French, Russian and Spanish texts are equally authentic, shall be deposited with the Secretary-General of the United Nations.

DONE at Paris this twelfth day of December two thousand and fifteen.

IN WITNESS WHEREOF, the undersigned, being duly authorized to that effect, have signed this Agreement.

Chapter 5

Conclusion

The Paris agreement focuses on confronting the climate crisis, and sending a critical message about the collective international obligation to turn away from fossil fuels. For the first time, poor and rich countries alike committed to curbing the greenhouse gas emissions that serve as the drivers for global warming by phasing out their reliance on carbon fuels in favor of renewable energy sources such as solar and wind.

The Paris accord marks a turning point for the planet. World leaders now acknowledge that climate change has and will continue to exact an incalculable toll on the world's people, especially the most vulnerable. It gives testament to the power of a mobilized global movement demanding universal and decisive action to avert a devastating climate breakdown.

The accord requires countries to develop and submit detailed plans to curb CO_2 emissions. States are required to submit to the ratchet mechanism, a framework that mandates them to return to the table every five years to review their emission reduction targets and spell out plans for progressively deeper cuts.

But the agreement's significant shortcomings underscore why this is only the beginning of a long and arduous battle. For example, a framework for transparency and compliance, through reporting and monitoring, has not yet been developed. And civil society will bear much of the burden of ensuring compliance with present commitments and in pressuring governments to act far more aggressively and equitably to avert the impending climate disaster.

Furthermore, the $100 billion a year in public and private financing pledged by wealthy countries to assist poorer countries to develop clean energy and ameliorate the hardships of rising sea levels and extreme weather is woefully inadequate. Besides, while the accord recognizes the differing responsibilities and obligations to address the crisis, individual financial commitments are not enforceable.

Activists are concerned that existing aid could be repackaged as climate aid, eviscerating the assistance these funds are intended to provide.

That's not all. Countries set a goal of keeping the average global temperature increase below 2 degrees Celsius above preindustrial levels, with a widely hailed aspiration to limit the rise to 1.5 degrees Celsius. A "1.5 to stay alive " campaign to lower the target was thought quixotic even in the face of mounting evidence that it is a tipping point for the climate, beyond which it could spin out of control. States agreed to balance carbon outputs and inputs in order to achieve net zero greenhouse gas emissions by the second half of the century. Yet experts say that the current commitments will result in an increase of nearly 3 degrees.

"The Paris agreement is a death sentence for many people," Pablo Solón, a former climate negotiator for Bolivia, told Democracy Now on Dec. 14. *"A world with temperature increases more than 3 degrees Celsius is a world where not everyone will survive."*

Since certain key provisions of the accord are not binding, political mobilization and naming and shaming will remain essential to prod nations to honor their commitments. Washington was instrumental in ensuring that the provisions are unenforceable, in part to avoid a bruising congressional showdown over ratification. But the lack of enforceability means that President Barack Obama's successor can easily walk back any commitments. The risk is highlighted by the Republican leadership's stubborn denial of climate change and the threat it poses to U.S. security.

The agreement contains other disappointing setbacks for the climate justice movement. Inclusion of the loss and damage clause acknowledges that rich, industrialized countries have developed at the expense of the planet's health by using more than their share of resources and emitting far more than their share of pollution while many poorer nations remain most vulnerable to the devastating effects of climate change. Yet the clause stipulates that it "does not involve or provide a basis for any liability or compensation." The carve-out leaves those harmed to rely on the goodwill of wealthier countries instead of creating enforceable rights.

Ultimately, parts of the Paris agreement could imperil the poor instead of ensuring their protection. For example, critics have labeled carbon-trading schemes to offset emissions as carbon colonization that has spurred land grabs and spawned conflict around the globe. A March 2014 report by the advocacy coalition Rights and Resources Initiative outlines the inadequacy of current legal protection for indigenous and local communities under carbon trading initiatives. World leaders declined to exclude large hydroelectric projects from sustainable climate initiatives despite a plea from more than 300 civil society organizations. In fact, human rights and protections for indigenous peoples were relegated to a nonbinding section of the agreement, weakening their ability to safeguard those who need it most.

Activists have denounced the corporate capture of the Paris talks, including sponsorship of the talks by corporations with dirty pollution records and vested interests in and track records of hampering de-carbonization of the economy. Corporations had an evident and outsize influence in exacerbating the climate crisis and thwarting reform attempts. Corporate malfeasance on the climate front was exemplified by the revelation that Exxon's 1977 research found burning fossil fuels was warming the planet and could harm humanity. Instead of working to ameliorate the predicted consequences, by the 1980s, Exxon had retrenched and invested its efforts in promoting climate denial.

"*The fossil fuel industry's lingering chokehold over U.S. politics leaves the Paris agreement a nearly empty vessel,*" Carroll Muffett, the president of the Center for International Environmental Law, said in statement on Dec. 12.

The Paris accord emanated from the combination of irrefutable scientific evidence of an imminent climate cataclysm, the persistent efforts of a vibrant and committed global climate movement and the dangers and harms already caused by extreme weather patterns. But the agreement alone cannot and will not save the planet. Activists should savor the progress but not pause to rest. Ensuring the accord amounts to more than hollow proclamations depends not on politicians but on the ability of the climate justice movement to sustain its vigilance and overcome resistance to the adaptations we all have to make, especially by those who profit most from damaging practices. In the end, our fates are all intertwined.

Reference

Battisti; David; Naylor, Rosamund L. (2009). *Historical warnings of future food insecurity with unprecedented seasonal heat.* Science 323 (5911): 240–4. Retrieved 13 April 2012.

United Nations Framework Convention on Climate Change (UNFCCC) (2011). *Status of Ratification of the Convention.* UNFCCC Secretariat: Bonn, Germany: UNFCCC. Most countries in the world are Parties to the United Nations Framework Convention on Climate Change (UNFCCC), which has adopted the 2 °C target. As of 25 November 2011, there are 195 parties (194 states and 1 regional economic integration organization (the European Union)) to the UNFCCC.

United Nations Framework Convention on Climate Change (UNFCCC) (2005). Sixth compilation and synthesis of initial national communications from Parties not included in Annex I to the Convention. Note by the secretariat. Executive summary (PDF). Geneva (Switzerland): United Nations Office at Geneva.

United Nations Framework Convention on Climate Change (UNFCCC) (2011). *Compilation and synthesis of fifth national communications.* Executive summary. Note by the secretariat" (PDF). Geneva (Switzerland): United Nations Office at Geneva.

Buis, Alan; Ramsayer, Kate; Rasmussen, Carol (12 November 2015). *A Breathing Planet, Off Balance.* NASA. Retrieved 13 November 2015.

St. Fleur, Nicholas (10 November 2015). *Atmospheric Greenhouse Gas Levels Hit Record, Report Says".* The New York Times. Retrieved 11 November 2015.

Ritter, Karl (9 November 2015). "*UK: In 1st, global temps average could be 1 degree C higher*". AP News. Retrieved 11 November 2015.

Kennedy, J.J.; et al. (2010). "*How do we know the world has warmed? in*: 2. Global Climate, in: State of the Climate in 2009". Bull. Amer. Meteor. Soc. 91 (7): 26.

Kennedy, C. (10 July 2012). "*ClimateWatch Magazine State of the Climate*: 2011 Global Sea Level". NOAA Climate Services Portal.

Rowan T. Sutton, Buwen Dong, Jonathan M. Gregory (2007). "*Land/sea warming ratio in response to climate change*: IPCC AR4 model results and comparison with observations". Geophysical Research Letters 34 (2). Retrieved 19 September 2007.

England, Matthew (February 2014). *Recent intensification of wind-driven circulation in the Pacific and the ongoing warming hiatus*. Nature Climate Change 4: 222–227.

Schmidt, Gavin (22 January 2015). "Thoughts on 2014 and ongoing temperature trends". RealClimate. Retrieved 4 September 2015.

Pew Center on Global Climate Change / Center for Climate and Energy Solutions (September 2006). "*Science Brief 1: The Causes of Global Climate Change*" (PDF). Arlington, Virginia, USA: Center for Climate and Energy Solutions., p.2

Issues and reasons behind the French offer to host the 21st Conference of the Parties on Climate Change 2015" . Ministry of Foreign Affairs. 22 May 2013. Retrieved 31 January 2014.

Firzli, M. Nicolas J. (September 2015). "Climate: Renewed Sense of Urgency in Washington and Beijing" (PDF). Analyse Financière. Retrieved 6 January 2016.

President Obama (12 December 2015). "*President Obama's Statement on Climate Change*" . White House Briefing Room. Retrieved 30 December 2015.

France confirmed as host of 2015 Climate Conference. Ministry of Foreign Affairs. 22 November 2013. Retrieved 31 January 2014.

Status of Ratification of the Convention. United Nations Framework Convention on Climate Change. Retrieved 15 Dec 2015.

Schedule of Events (PDF). United Nations Framework Convention on Climate Change. Retrieved 12 November 2013.

Chappel, Bill (12 December 2015). "*Nearly 200 Nations Adopt Climate Agreement At COP21 Talks In Paris*".NPR . Retrieved 12 December 2015.

Milman, Oliver (12 December 2015). *James Hansen, father of climate change awareness, calls Paris talks 'a fraud'*. The Guardian (London, England). Retrieved 14 December 2015.

Pengelly, Martin (December 12, 2015). *Obama praises Paris climate deal as 'tribute to American leadership*. The Guardian (London, England). Retrieved.

Kinver, Mark (14 December 2015). COP21: *What does the Paris climate agreement mean for me?* BBC News . BBC. Retrieved 14 December 2015.

Reguly, Eric (14 December 2015). *"Paris climate accord marks shift toward low-carbon economy"*. Globe and Mail (Toronto, Canada). Retrieved 14 December 2015.

Davenport, Coral (12 December 2015). *"Nations Approve Landmark Climate Accord in Paris"* . New York Times. New York Times. Retrieved 14 December 2015.

Andrew Pearce (6 December 2015). Jeffrey Sachs: *Fund Managers Have a Duty to Dump Fossil Fuels"* . Financial News . Retrieved 16 December 2015.

John Vidal (13 December 2015). *"Paris Climate Agreement 'May Signal End of Fossil Fuel Era'"* . The Guardian. Retrieved 16 December 2015.

World Mayors and Municipal Leaders Declaration on Climate Change" (PDF). Archive.iclei.org. Retrieved 15 November 2015.

European capital and large cities for climate action en route to COP 21 (PDF). Stadtentwicklung.berlin.de. Retrieved 15 November 2015.

World Summit of Regions for Climate. Regions-climate.org. 11 October 2014. Retrieved 15 November 2015.

Indigenous Peoples of Africa Co-ordinating Committee. IPACC. Retrieved 15 November 2015.

United Nations Declaration on the Rights of Indigenous Peoples" (PDF). Un.org. Retrieved 15 November 2015.

www.ingramcontent.com/pod-product-compliance
Lightning Source LLC
Chambersburg PA
CBHW062050280526
45788CB00003B/1170